Essential English

Written by
Christopher Warnasch

Edited by
Laura Riggio

LIVING LANGUAGE®

Oct 2013

Published in the United States by Living Language, an imprint of Random House, Inc.

www.livinglanguage.com

Editor: Laura Riggio
Production Editor: Ciara Robinson
Production Manager: Tom Marshall
Interior Design: Sophie Chin
Illustrations: Sophie Chin

First Edition

ISBN: 978-0-307-97233-0

This book is available at special discounts for bulk purchases for sales promotions or premiums. Special editions, including personalized covers, excerpts of existing books, and corporate imprints, can be created in large quantities for special needs. For more information, write to Special Markets/ Premium Sales, 1745 Broadway, MD 3-1, New York, New York 10019 or e-mail specialmarkets@ randomhouse.com.

PRINTED IN THE UNITED STATES OF AMERICA

10 9 8 7 6 5 4 3 2 1

Acknowledgments

Thanks to the Living Language team: Amanda D'Acierno, Christopher Warnasch, Suzanne McQuade, Laura Riggio, Erin Quirk, Amanda Munoz, Fabrizio LaRocca, Siobhan O'Hare, Sophie Chin, Pat Stango, Sue Daulton, Alison Skrabek, Carolyn Roth, Ciara Robinson, and Tom Marshall.

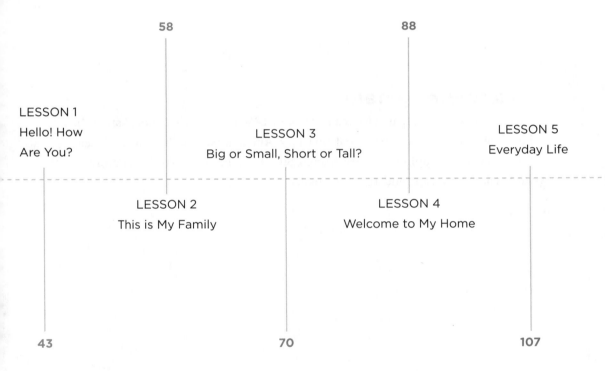

COURSE

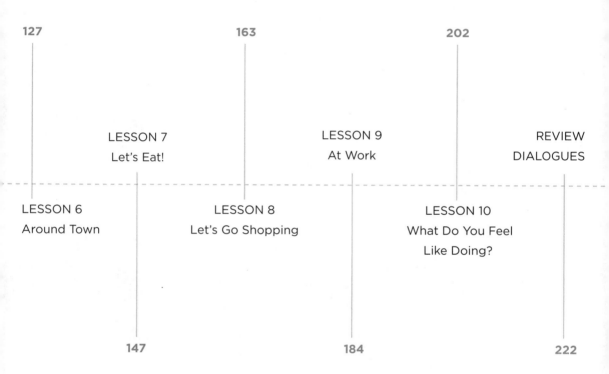
OUTLINE

Introduction: English

Welcome to *Living Language Essential English*! This is a basic course in English for speakers of any language. You'll learn new vocabulary and grammar through context, with carefully arranged examples that will make the rules of English clear to you. Because the context and examples will make meanings clear, you don't need translations. But if you don't understand a word from context, you can look it up online or in a dictionary.

LESSONS

There are ten lessons in *Essential English* that will introduce you to the vocabulary and basic grammar that you'll need to get by in a range of situations. Each lesson includes:

Welcome: a short introduction that tells you what the lesson is about

Vocabulary Builder 1 and 2: important words and phrases related to the topic of the lesson

Vocabulary Practice 1 and 2: practice that focuses on the new vocabulary

Grammar Builder 1 and 2: simple explanations and examples of important grammar

Work Out 1 and 2: practice exercises that focus on the grammar and vocabulary from the lesson

Bring It All Together: a dialogue or short reading that uses the vocabulary and grammar you've learned in the lesson

Drive It Home: an important practice designed to make English grammar automatic

Parting Words: a summary of what you've learned in the lesson

Take It Further: extra sections that give you more information, vocabulary, or explanation

WORD RECALL

Word Recall sections appear in between lessons and remind you of important vocabulary from the previous lesson.

QUIZZES

Quiz 1 is after Lesson 5, and Quiz 2 is after Lesson 10. Grade yourself on the quizzes to see what you need to review.

REVIEW DIALOGUES

There are five review dialogues at the end of the course that will help you learn everyday spoken English. Each dialogue has comprehension questions. Don't forget to use your dictionary if you need help with any new vocabulary.

PROGRESS BAR

The Progress Bar tells you where you are in the course.

AUDIO

Look for this symbol ⊙ in each lesson. It will tell you which track to listen to for each section that has audio. If you don't see the symbol, then there isn't any audio for that section.

GRAMMAR SUMMARY

At the end of the book, you'll find a grammar summary, which covers all of the important grammar that you'll learn in *Essential English*.

FREE ONLINE TOOLS

Go to **www.livinglanguage.com/languagelab** for your free online tools. There are flashcards with images and audio, as well as interactive review games.

Introducción: Español

¡Bienvenidos al curso de inglés esencial *Living Language Essential English*! Es un curso de inglés básico para hablantes de cualquier idioma. Con este sistema aprenderá vocabulario y gramática en su contexto natural, usando ejemplos muy bien seleccionados que le hará entender las reglas del inglés. Como el contexto y los ejemplos le dejarán claro su significado, no serán necesarias las traducciones. Claro que si no logra entender del todo alguna palabra mediante su contexto, la podrá buscar en su diccionario o en internet.

LESSONS

Hay diez lecciones en el curso *Essential English* que introducen el vocabulario y la gramática básica que necesitará para desenvolverse en una variedad de situaciones. Cada lección viene con las siguientes secciones:

Vocabulary Builder 1 and 2: Un constructor de vocabulario donde encontrará las palabras y frases más importantes relacionadas al tema de la lección

Vocabulary Practice 1 and 2: Práctica de vocabulario donde se enfoca el vocabulario nuevo

Grammar Builder 1 and 2: Un constructor de gramática con ejemplos y explicaciones simples de los conceptos gramaticales que necesita aprender

Work Out 1 and 2: Una serie de ejercicios de práctica con enfoque en la gramática y el vocabulario de cada lección

Bring It All Together: Un corto diálogo o lectura donde se junta el vocabulario y la gramática de la lección

Drive It Home: Un importante ejercicio adicional donde se reitera la gramática inglesa, una práctica diseñada para que el estudiante responda a la gramática de forma automática

Parting Words: Nuestras palabras de despedida, donde resumimos lo aprendido en la lección

Take It Further: Donde expandimos el conocimiento con secciones adicionales que brindan más información, explicaciones o vocabulario

WORD RECALL

Las secciones del Word Recall (Repaso de Palabras) aparecen entre una lección y otra para repasar el vocabulario de lecciones anteriores y así no olvidarlo.

QUIZZES

La primera prueba aparece después de la Lección 5, la segunda prueba aparece después de la Lección 10. Califíque su propia prueba con la clave de respuestas para ver qué conceptos o vocabulario necesita repasar más.

REVIEW DIALOGUES

Hay cinco diálogos de repaso al final del curso que le ayudarán a aprender el inglés coloquial de todos los días. Cada diálogo viene con sus preguntas de comprensión de lectura. No se olvide de usar su diccionario si necesita ayuda con el vocabulario nuevo.

PROGRESS BAR

La Barra de Progreso indica en dónde se encuentra dentro del curso.

AUDIO

Busque este símbolo ⊙ en cada lección. Le dirá cuál grabación tendrá que escuchar para cada una de las secciones que vienen con audio. Si no ve el símbolo, entonces no hay audio en esa sección.

GRAMMAR SUMMARY

Al final del libro, encontrará un resumen gramatical que cubre toda la gramática importante que aprenderá en el curso *Essential English*.

FREE ONLINE TOOLS

Visite **www.livinglanguage.com/languagelab** para adquirir otros recursos, contenido y herramientas gratis. Encontrará fichas de vocabulario con imágenes y audio, además de juegos interactivos de repaso.

介绍：中文

感谢您购买 *Living Language* 基础英语教材。这是一套为任何语言读者准备的基础英语教材。您将通过教材的课文内容学习新的词汇和语法，并通过精心安排的范例弄清英语的规则。由于课文内容和范例的意思明确，您不需要翻译。但是，如果您不明白课文中某个单词的意思，您可以在网上或字典中查找一下。

LESSONS

在基础英语中有十篇课文，将介绍您在一些情况下需要的词汇和基本语法。每篇课文包含：

Welcome: 简短地向您介绍这篇课文的内容

Vocabulary Builder 1 and 2: 与课文相关的重要词汇和短语

Vocabulary Practice 1 and 2: 着重于新词汇的练习

Grammar Builder 1 and 2: 关于重要语法的简单解释与范例

Work Out 1 and 2: 着重于课文中语法和词汇的练习

Bring It All Together: 对话或一段短文，运用您在课文中学习的词汇和语法

Drive It Home: 为自如地运用英语语法而设计的重要练习

Parting Words: 概括您在这篇课文中所学的内容

Take It Further: 给您更多信息，词汇与解释的额外章节

WORD RECALL

词汇记忆章节出现在两篇课文的中间以帮助您回忆在前一篇课文中学习到的重要词汇。

QUIZZES

测验 1 在第五课后，测验 2 在第十课后。请在测验后给自己评分，以此来检查哪些部分需要再复习一下。

REVIEW DIALOGUES

在整个课程的最后有五篇复习对话以帮助您学习日常英语口语。每篇对话有阅读理解的问题。如您对某个新单词需要帮助，请别忘了使用您的字典。

PROGRESS BAR

进程表将告诉您在整个课程的学习进程。

AUDIO

在每篇课文中看到这个符号 ▶，表示在此有音频的章节以及需要收听的音频轨道。如果您没有看到这个符号，则表示该章节没有音频资料。

GRAMMAR SUMMARY

在本书的最后, 您将找语法概要。该语法概要涵盖所有您在基础英语中所学到的重要语法。

FREE ONLINE TOOLS

请前往 **www.livinglanguage.com/languagelab** 查询您的免费在线工具。这些免费在线工具包括具有图像和音频的记忆卡，以及互动复习游戏。

Introdução: Português

Bem-vindo ao *Living Language Essential English*! Este curso básico de inglês foi feito para pessoas que falam qualquer idioma. Através de exemplos cuidadosamente selecionados e do contexto das lições, você aprenderá vocabulário e gramática. E como estes simplificam a compreensão das regras do inglês não há necessidade de traduções. Se, ainda assim, você não entender uma palavra, você pode procurar o significado online ou em um dicionário.

LESSONS

Lessons são as dez lições do *Essential English* que introduzem a gramática e o vocabulário básico que você precisa saber para se sair bem em uma série de situações. Cada lição inclui:

Welcome: Bem-vindo é a seção onde você encontra uma breve introdução descrevendo o conteúdo das lições.

Vocabulary Builder 1 and 2: Essas seções introduzem palavras e frases importantes relacionadas ao tema da lição.

Vocabulary Practice 1 and 2: Aqui você encontra exercícios práticos que consolidam o novo vocabulário.

Grammar Builder 1 and 2: Aqui você encontra explicações e exemplos simplificados com importantes pontos gramaticais

Work Out 1 and 2: Esses são exercícios práticos que consolidam o vocabulário e a gramática da lição.

Bring It All Together: Nessa seção você vai ler um diálogo ou texto breve que usa o vocabulário e a gramática que você aprendeu na lição.

Drive It Home: Esse exercício é programado especificamente para tornar a gramática inglesa automática.

Parting Words: Aqui você tem um resumo de tudo aquilo que você aprendeu na lição.

Take It Further: Essas seções adicionais dão mais informações, vocabulário ou explicações.

WORD RECALL

As seções intituladas Word Recall aparecem entre uma lição e outra para você revisar o vocabulário mais importante das lições anteriores.

QUIZZES

O primeiro teste chamado Quiz 1 vem após a lição 5, e o segundo, Quiz 2, vem depois da lição 10. Você poderá se auto avaliar verificando se há necessidade de uma revisão.

REVIEW DIALOGUES

Na seção Review Dialogues no final do curso, você vai encontrar cinco diálogos para revisão que ajudarão você aprender o inglês falado no dia a dia. Cada diálogo vem acompanhado de perguntas para testar a sua compreensão. Não deixe de usar o dicionário se você precisar de ajuda com alguma palavra nova.

PROGRESS BAR

O Progress Bar, ou barra de progresso, mostra em que parte do curso você está.

AUDIO

Procure este símbolo ⊙ em cada lição. Ele informará o número da faixa você deve ouvir na seção que possui recurso oral. Se uma seção não tem esse símbolo é porque ela não tem um componente de áudio.

GRAMMAR SUMMARY

No final do livro você vai encontrar um resumo gramatical intitulado Grammar Summary, que cobre toda a gramática que você vai aprender no *Essential English*.

FREE ONLINE TOOLS

Encontre várias ferramentas gratuitas no **www.livinglanguage.com/languagelab**. Lá você vai ter acesso a recursos audiovisuais assim como jogos interativos para revisão.

परिचय: हिंदी

Living Language Essential English आपका स्वागत करता है। यह एक आसान पाठ्यक्रम है जिसे पढ़कर किसी भी भाषा के जानकार अंग्रेज़ी सीख सकते हैं। इसमें आप नयी शब्दावली और व्याकरण सीखेंगे। साथ ही इसमें रचे उदाहरणों द्वारा आपको अंग्रेज़ी भाषा के नियम भी स्पष्ट रूप से जानने को मिलेंगे। इसमें प्रयोग किये गए उदहारण तथा सन्दर्भों के द्वारा आपको अर्थ स्पष्ट होते जायेंगे तथा आपको अनुवादों की आवश्यकता नहीं रहेगी। लेकिन, यदि आपको किसी शब्द का अर्थ उसके सन्दर्भ में किये गए प्रयोग से समझ न आये, तो आप शब्दकोश या ऑनलाइन वेबसाइट का प्रयोग कर सकते हैं।

LESSONS

Essential English में दस पाठ हैं। ये पाठ आपको विभिन्न स्थितियों में प्रयोग होनेवाले शब्द तथा व्याकरण की जानकारी देंगे। प्रत्येक पाठ में निम्नलिखित अध्याय सम्मिलित हैं:

Welcome: पाठ का संक्षिप्त परिचय

Vocabulary Builder 1 and 2: पाठ से सम्बंधित शब्दावली और व्याकरण

Vocabulary Practice 1 and 2: नवीन शब्दावली पर केन्द्रित अभ्यास

Grammar Builder 1 and 2: आवश्यक व्याकरण के सरल वर्णन और उदाहरण

Work Out 1 and 2: पाठ में प्रयोग किये गए शब्द तथा व्याकरण पर केन्द्रित अभ्यासक्रम

Bring It All Together: पाठ में सीखे हुए शब्दावली और व्याकरण का संक्षिप्त संवाद या पठन

Drive It Home: अंग्रेज़ी व्याकरण का स्वतंत्र तथा स्वचलित उपयोग करने हेतु बनाया गया एक विशेष अभ्यासक्रम

Parting Words: पाठ का सारांश

Take It Further: अधिक जानकारी, नवीन शब्द तथा वर्णन युक्त अतिरिक्त संभाग

WORD RECALL

ये संभाग पाठ्यक्रम में बीच बीच में आयेंगे। वे पिछले पाठ के महत्वपूर्ण शब्दों का पुनः स्मरण करवाएंगे।

QUIZZES

क्विज़ या प्रश्नावली १ पाठ ५ के बाद, और क्विज़ या प्रश्नावली २ पाठ १० के बाद आते हैं। इस प्रश्नोत्तरी से आप अपने अब तक के ज्ञान को स्वयं परख सकते हैं।

REVIEW DIALOGUES

पाठ्यक्रम के अंत में पांच संवाद हैं जिनके पुनः स्मरण से आप सरल बोलचाल की अंग्रेज़ी सीख सकते हैं। प्रत्येक संवाद में बोध हेतु प्रश्न दिए गए हैं। यदि कोई नए शब्द समझ न आयें तो शब्दकोष की मदद लेना न भूलें।

PROGRESS BAR

प्रोग्रेस बार या प्रगति माप की मदद से आप पाठ्यक्रम में अपनी प्रगति का स्तर जान सकते हैं।

AUDIO

प्रत्येक पाठ में ▶ का चिन्ह है। यह चिन्ह श्रव्य विभाग की पहचान है। यदि किसी विभाग में यह चिन्ह नहीं है तो वह विभाग श्रव्य नहीं है।

GRAMMAR SUMMARY

Essential English पाठ्यक्रम में सिखाये गए महत्त्वपूर्ण व्याकरण का सारांश आपको पुस्तक के अंत में मिलेगा।

FREE ONLINE TOOLS

अपने नि:शुल्क ऑनलाइन साधन **www.livinglanguage.com/languagelab** से प्राप्त करें। इन साधनों में छवियाँ तथा श्रव्य फ्लाशकार्ड और संवादात्मक निरीक्षण हेतु खेल तथा प्रश्नावली सम्मिलित हैं।

Présentation: Français

Bienvenue au *Living Language Essential English*! Ceci est un cours d'anglais basique quelle que soit la langue que vous pratiquez. Vous allez acquérir le vocabulaire et la grammaire dans un contexte, à l'aide d'exemples élaborés avec soin qui vous faciliteront la compréhension des règles de l'anglais. Grâce à des exemples mis en situation dans un contexte clairement compréhensible, vous n'aurez pas besoin de traduction. Si toutefois vous ne comprenez pas un mot dans son contexte, vous pouvez toujours le rechercher en ligne ou dans un dictionnaire.

LESSONS

Essential English vous propose 10 leçons pour acquérir le vocabulaire et la grammaire de base que vous pourrez utiliser dans des circonstances très variées. Chaque leçon comprend:

Welcome: une courte introduction qui vous présente le thème de la leçon.

Vocabulary Builder 1 and 2: mots et phrases importants liés au contenu de la leçon.

Vocabulary Practice 1 and 2: exercice pratique portant sur le vocabulaire de la leçon.

Grammar Builder 1 and 2: explications simples et exemples sur les points de grammaire importants.

Work Out 1 and 2: exercices pratiques réactivant le vocabulaire et la grammaire abordés dans la leçon.

Bring It All Together: dialogue ou courte lecture utilisant le vocabulaire et la grammaire que vous venez d'apprendre.

Drive It Home: exercice important pour acquérir des automatismes dans la pratique de la grammaire anglaise.

Parting Words: bilan de ce que vous avez appris dans la leçon.

Take It Further: un supplément, avec d'avantage d'informations, de vocabulaire ou d'explications.

WORD RECALL

Vous trouverez les pages « Rappel du Vocabulaire » entre deux leçons pour vous remémorer le vocabulaire important de la leçon précédente.

QUIZZES

Après la leçon 5, et après la leçon 10, les quizzes 1 et 2 vous permettront de faire une auto-évaluation de vos acquis afin de pointer ce que vous devez réviser.

REVIEW DIALOGUES

Il y a 5 dialogues de révision à la fin du cours pour vous aider à apprendre l'anglais de tous les jours. Chaque dialogue comporte des questions de compréhension.

N'oubliez pas d'utiliser le dictionnaire si vous avez besoin d'aide pour le vocabulaire nouveau.

PROGRESS BAR

Elle vous dira votre niveau dans le cours.

AUDIO

Cherchez le symbole ⊙ dans chaque leçon. Il vous indiquera le numéro de la piste à écouter. Si vous ne voyez pas ce symbole, c'est qu'il n'y a pas de piste audio pour cette section.

GRAMMAR SUMMARY

A la fin du livre vous trouverez une partie grammaire qui reprend tous les points importants étudiés dans *Essential English*, ainsi qu'un index du vocabulaire vous indiquant dans quelle leçon dans quelle leçon le mot est apparu pour la première fois.

FREE ONLINE TOOLS

Allez à **www.livinglanguage.com/languagelab** pour accéder à vos outils en ligne gratuits. Vous y trouverez des fiches audiovisuelles, ainsi que des jeux de révision interactifs.

イントロダクション：日本語

Living Language Essential English へようこそ！このプログラムは英語を学びたい全ての人を対象とした入門編です。入念に練られた豊富な用例を通して、語彙や文法を分かりやすく学んでいくことができます。明解な用例がふんだんに盛り込まれているので、言葉や文の意味はおのずと分かるようにできています。ですから和訳を参照する必要はありません。けれどももし意味が明確でない場合はネットや辞書で調べてください。

LESSONS

Essential English は全10課から構成されており、様々なシチュエーションで役立つ語彙や基本文法を紹介していきます。それぞれの課には以下の項目が盛り込まれています。

Welcome：本課で学習する内容の紹介

Vocabulary Builder 1 and 2：本課のトピックに関連した重要語句

Vocabulary Practice 1 and 2：新出語句を中心とした演習

Grammar Builder 1 and 2：重要文法事項の説明と用例

Work Out 1 and 2：新出文法や語句を中心とした演習

Bring It All Together：新しく学んだ文法を使った会話や文章

Drive It Home：何も考えることなく文法がすらすらと出てくるようになるための重要な演習

Parting Words：本課で学習したことのまとめ

Take It Further：もう少し深くつっこんで学びたい人のための情報源

WORD RECALL

各課の終わりには Word Recall があり、前課で学習した重要単語を忘れないようにするために設けられています。

QUIZZES

Lesson 5 の後に Quiz 1、Lesson 10 の後に Quiz 2 が設けられています。自己採点してもう一度復習するべき点を確認してください。

REVIEW DIALOGUES

本書の終わりには日常英会話の学習に役立つ 5 つの会話が用意されています。それぞれの会話には内容の理解度を確認するためのテストがついています。分からない新出単語があったら辞書を引きましょう。

PROGRESS BAR

Progress Bar で本書における学習の進み具合を確認することができます。

AUDIO

▶ のマークは音声がCDで聞けることを表しています。CDのトラックナンバーも一緒に記載されています。▶ のマークが見当たらない場合は、そのセクションのオーディオはないということです。

GRAMMAR SUMMARY

巻末には Grammar Summary があり、*Essential English* で網羅されている全ての文法事項を確認することができます。

FREE ONLINE TOOLS

こちらのページでは、学習に役立つ様々なツールを無料で利用することができます。**www.livinglanguage.com/languagelab** 画像と音声付きのバーチャル単語カードや学習内容の理解度を確認できるゲームが用意されています。

Wstęp: Język Polski

Witamy w *Living Language Essential English*! Jest to kurs języka angielskiego dla
początkujących, niezależnie od ich języka ojczystego. Nauczysz się z nami nowego
słownictwa i gramatyki w kontekście, poprzez starannie dobrane przykłady, które
spowodują, że zasady języka angielskiego staną się dla Ciebie w pełni zrozumiałe.
Ponieważ kontekst i przykłady sprawią, że będzie Ci łatwo zrozumieć lekcje,
tłumaczenia nie będą Ci potrzebne. Jeżeli jednak nie zrozumiesz jakiegoś słowa
z kontekstu, możesz znaleźć je w internecie lub w słowniku.

LESSONS

Essential English składa się z dziesięciu lekcji, które zaznajomią Cię ze
słownictwem i podstawową gramatyką potrzebną by poradzić sobie
w różnorodnych sytuacjach. Każda lekcja zawiera:

Welcome: krótki wstęp, który opisuje o czym jest lekcja

Vocabulary Builder 1 and 2: ważne słowa i wyrażenia związane z tematem lekcji

Vocabulary Practice 1 and 2: ćwiczenia skoncentrowane na utrwaleniu nowego
słownictwa

Grammar Builder 1 and 2: proste opisy i przykłady ważnych zagadnień
gramatycznych

Work Out 1 and 2: praktyczne ćwiczenia skoncentrowane na gramatyce i słownictwie z danej lekcji

Bring It All Together: dialog lub krótka czytanka zawierająca słownictwo i gramatykę, której nauczyłeś się w danej lekcji

Drive It Home: ważne ćwiczenia zaprojektowane w celu zautomatyzowania wiedzy o gramatyce angielskiej

Parting Words podsumowanie materiału, którego nauczyłeś się w danej lekcji

Take It Further: dodatkowe sekcje oferujące więcej informacji, słownictwa, lub wyjaśnień.

WORD RECALL

Sekcje Przypomnienie Słownictwa pojawiają się pomiędzy lekcjami, aby przypomnieć Ci o ważnych słowach z poprzedniej lekcji.

QUIZZES

Test 1 znajduje się po Lekcji 5, a Test 2 po Lekcji 10. Testy te pozwolą Ci sprawdzić swoją wiedzę i ocenić, co potrzebujesz powtórzyć.

REVIEW DIALOGUES

Na końcu kursu znajdziesz pięć powtórkowych dialogów, które pomogą Ci nauczyć się codziennych konwersacji w języku angielskim.

PROGRESS BAR

Wskaźnik Postępów pokazuje Ci, w którym miejscu kursu jesteś.

AUDIO

Szukaj symbolu ⊙ w każdej lekcji. Wskaże Ci on, którego nagrania słuchać dla każdej sekcji, która ma pliki dźwiękowe.

GRAMMAR SUMMARY

Na końcu książki znajdziesz Podsumowanie Gramatyki, które zbiera wszystkie ważne zagadnienia gramatyczne omawiane w kursie *Essential English*.

FREE ONLINE TOOLS

Twoje darmowe pomoce do nauki języka angielskiego możesz znaleźć na stronie internetowej **www.livinglanguage.com/languagelab**. Dostępne są tam karty z nagraniami i obrazkami oraz interaktywne gry do powtórzenia i utrwalenia wiedzy.

소개: 한국어

*Living Language Essential English*에 오신 걸 환영합니다! 이 코스는 영어를 모국어로 쓰지 않는 사람들을 위한 기본 코스입니다. 여러분은 영어의 규칙을 명백하게 보여줄 잘 정리된 예제들과 문맥을 통해서 새로운 어휘와 문법을 배우게 될 것입니다. 주어진 문맥과 예들이 의미를 분명하게 해주기때문에, 여러분은 번역이 필요치 않습니다. 하지만 문맥에서 단어를 이해하지 못 할 경우 인터넷이나 사전에서 단어를 찾아보셔도 됩니다.

LESSONS

*Essential English*는 여러 가지 상황에서 꼭 필요한 단어들과 기본 문법을 소개하는 총 열 개의 레슨을 제공합니다. 각 레슨은 다음과 같이 구성됩니다.

Welcome: 학습 내용을 설명하는 짤막한 소개

Vocabulary Builder 1 and 2: 학습 주제에 관련된 중요 단어와 문구들

Vocabulary Practice 1 and 2: 새로운 단어에 초점을 맞춘 연습

Grammar Builder 1 and 2: 중요한 문법의 간단한 설명과 예제

Work Out 1 and 2: 레슨에서 배운 문법과 단어에 초점을 둔 연습 문제

Bring it All Together: 레슨에서 배운 단어와 문법을 이용한 대화 혹은 짧은 글 읽기

Drive it Home: 영어 문법의 자동 습득을 위해 고안된 중요 연습

Parting Words: 레슨에서 배운 내용 요약

Take it Further: 추가 정보, 단어 및 설명을 제공하는 부록

WORD RECALL

Word Recall섹션은 레슨들 사이마다 주어지며 그 전 학습에서 배운 중요한 단어들을 상기시킵니다.

QUIZZES

Quiz 1은 Lesson 5, Quiz 2는 Lesson 10 후에 있습니다. 무엇을 다시 복습해야 하는지 알기 위해 문제를 푼 후 스스로 채점하기 바랍니다.

REVIEW DIALOGUES

코스 마지막에 일일 상용 영어를 위한 다섯 개의 복습 회화가 있습니다. 각 회화는 이해력 문제를 제공합니다. 모르는 새 단어에 대해 도움이 필요하면 사전을 찾아보기 바랍니다.

PROGRESS BAR

향상 도표는 여러분이 배우는 과정에서 어디쯤 와 있는지 알려줍니다.

AUDIO

각 레슨에서 기호 ▶를 찾아보세요. 그 기호는 오디오를 포함한 각 섹션에서 어느 트랙을 들어야 하는지 알려줍니다. 만약 이 기호가 보이지 않는다면, 그 섹션에는 오디오가 포함되어 있지 않습니다.

GRAMMAR SUMMARY

책 마지막에 여러분이*Essential English*에서 배우게 될 중요한 문법을 정리한 Grammar Summary이 있습니다.

FREE ONLINE TOOLS

www.livinglanguage.com/languagelab 에서 무료 온라인 도움을 받으세요. 그림과 음성을 포함한 플래쉬 카드와 리뷰 게임이 제공됩니다.

مقدمة: اللغة العربية

رحبا بكم *Living Language Essential English*! إنّها الدورة الأساسية في اللغة الإنجليزية للمتحدثين من كُلّ اللغات. في ستتعلّم مفردات جديدة والنحو من خلال حالات و مواضيع موجودة في الدرس مع أمثلة مختارة بعناية لتجعل قواعد اللغة الإنجليزية واضحة لك. بما أنّ الأمثلة واضحة المعاني لن تحتاج لأي ترجمة. ولكن إذ لم تفهم كلمة من الموضوع، يمكنك البحث عنها على الإنترنت أو في القاموس.

LESSONS

هناك عشرة دروس في اللغة الإنجليزية الأساسية التي ستعرض لكم المفردات والقواعد الأساسية التي ستحتاج إليْها في مجموعة من الحالات كل درس يحتوي على ما يلي:

Welcome مرحبا: مقدمة قصيرة تخبرك عن ما يحتوي الدرس.

Vocabulary Builder 1 and 2: الكلمات و العبارات الهامة المرتبطة بموضوع الدرس.

Vocabulary Practice 1 and 2: الممارسة التي تركز على المفردات الجديدة.

Grammar Builder 1 and 2: تفسيرات بسيطة وأمثلة للقواعد الهامة.

Work Out 1 and 2: التمارين التي تركز على قواعد اللغة ومفردات الدرس.

Bring It All Together: القراءة أو الحوار القصير الذي يستخدم المفردات والقواعد التي تعلمتها في الدرس.

Drive It Home: ممارسة هامة تهدف إلى جعل اللغة الإنجليزية و النحو أوتوماتيكي.

اللغة العربية

Parting Words: خلاصة من ما تعلمته في الدرس.

Take It Further: أجزاء إضافية تعطيك المزيد من المعلومات ، المفردات أو التفسير.

WORD RECALL

نذكر في هـذا الجزء الكلمـات التي ظهرت في الـدروس والمفردات الهامـة من الدرس السابق.

QUIZZES

الاختبار 1 يوجد بعد الدرس 5، و الإختبار 2 بعد الدرس 10. تدرّب مع الاختبارات لمعرفة ما تحتاج مراجعته.

REVIEW DIALOGUES

هناك خمس حوارات في نهاية الدرس التي سـوف تسـاعدك على تعلم اللغة الإنجليزية التي نستعمل في الحياة اليومية. بعد كل حوار سـتجيب على أسئلة فهم الحوار. لا تنس أن تستخدم القاموس إذا كنت بحاجة إلى مساعدة مع أي من المفردات الجديدة.

PROGRESS BAR

يخبرك عن تقدمك في هذه الدورة.

AUDIO

في كل درس إبحث عن هـذا الرمز ⏵. سـيخبرك عـن المقطع الذي يجـب عليك أن تسـتمع إليه والذي يحتوي على تسـجيل. إذا لم تشـاهده ⏵. إذن ليس هناك أي صوت لهذا المقطع.

GRAMMAR SUMMARY

في نهاية الكتاب سـتجد ملخصا نحوي يركز على القواعد الهامة التي تعلّمتها في اللغة الإنجليزية الأساسية.

FREE ONLINE TOOLS

إنتقل إلى www.livinglanguage.com/languagelab مجانـا على الأنترنيت مع صور و صوت وكذالك ألعاب تفاعلية للمراجعة.

Введение: русский язык

Добро пожаловать в *Living Language Essential English*! Это начальный курс, написанный для всех желающих независимо от их родного языка. Все новые слова, выражения и грамматика вводятся в контексте, на тщательно подобранных примерах, наглядно иллюстрирующих правила английского языка. Контекста и примеров достаточно, чтобы понять смысл, не прибегая к переводу. В случае необходимости Вы всегда сможете найти значение каждого слова онлайн или в словаре.

LESSONS

Essential English состоит из десяти уроков, в которых Вы ознакомитесь с ключевыми словами, выражениями и грамматическими конструкциями необходимыми для общения в самых различных ситуациях. Каждый урок включает в себя следующие компоненты:

Welcome: краткое вступление, знакомящее Вас с темой урока

Vocabulary Builder 1 and 2: основные слова и выражения, относящиеся к теме урока

Vocabulary Practice 1 and 2: практика на новые слова и выражения

Grammar Builder 1 and 2: простые объяснения и примеры основных грамматических конструкций

Work Out 1 and 2: практические упражнения на грамматику и словарный запас данного урока

Bring It All Together: диалог или короткий текст, в котором использованы слова и грамматика из данного урока

Drive It Home: важное упражнение на закрепление конкретных грамматических конструкций

Parting Words: краткое содержание всего, что Вы выучили в данном уроке

Take It Further: разделы с дополнительной информацией, расширенным словарным запасом и более подробными объяснениями

WORD RECALL

Раздел Word Recall помещён между уроками с целью повторения важных слов и выражений из предшествующих уроков

QUIZZES

Quiz 1 следует после Lesson 5, а Quiz 2 – после Lesson 10. Вы сами проверяете свои контрольные работы, ставите себе оценку и таким образом узнаёте, нужно ли Вам что-либо повторить.

REVIEW DIALOGUES

В заключение курса помещаются пять диалогов, которые помогут Вам приобрести навыки современного разговорного английского языка. Все диалоги сопровождаются вопросами на понимание. При чтении диалогов Вы можете в случае необходимости пользоваться словарём.

PROGRESS BAR

Шкала прогресса показывает Вам, на каком этапе курса вы находитесь в данный момент.

AUDIO

В каждом уроке вы увидите значок ⊙. Им отмечены те части урока, которые сопровождаются аудиозаписью, а также указан соответствующий номер аудиотрека.

GRAMMAR SUMMARY

В конце книги вы найдёте Grammar Summary (краткий обзор грамматики), в котором содержатся основные грамматические правила, пройденные Вами в *Essential English*.

FREE ONLINE TOOLS

На вебсайте **www.livinglanguage.com/languagelab** Вы найдёте бесплатные учебные пособия. Там есть словарные карточки с картинками, аудиозаписи, а также интерактивные игры на повторение.

Introduzione: Italiano

Benvenuto a *Living Language Essential English*!, un corso di base di lingua inglese per tutti, a prescindere dalla tua lingua madre. Imparerai il vocabolario e la grammatica inglese con un metodo "contestuale", ovvero con esempi accuratamente organizzati che renderanno semplici le regole della lingua inglese. Dato che il contesto e gli esempi avranno significati molto chiari, non avrai bisogno di traduzioni. Ciò detto, se non capirai una parola dal contesto, potrai sempre usare un dizionario o cercare la parola on-line.

LESSONS

Le dieci lezioni di *Essential English* ti introdurranno al vocabolario e alla grammatica di base di cui avrai bisogno per parlare inglese in una vasta gamma di situazioni. Ogni lezione comprende:

Welcome: una breve introduzione su ciò che imparerai nella lezione.

Vocabulary Builder 1 and 2: include le parole e le frasi importanti legate al vocabolario acquisito nella lezione

Vocabulary Practice 1 and 2: pratica che si concentra sul nuovo vocabolario

Grammatica Builder 1 and 2: spiegazioni ed esempi semplici per concetti importanti della grammatica

Work Out 1 and 2: esercizi sulla grammatica e sul vocabolario della lezione

Bring It All Together: un breve brano di lettura o un dialogo che utilizza il vocabolario e la grammatica che hai imparato durante la lezione

Drive It Home: un'importante modello progettato per rendere automatico l'uso della grammatica inglese

Parting Words: un riassunto di ciò che hai imparato durante la lezione

Take It Further: una sezione extra che ti da ulteriori informazioni, vocabolario e spiegazioni

WORD RECALL

La sezione Word Recall appare tra una lezione e un'altra e serve per farti ricordare i vocaboli importanti della lezione precedente.

QUIZZES

Il Quiz 1 è dopo Lezione 5, Quiz e 2 è dopo la lezione 10. Usa i risultati dei quiz per sapere cosa devi ripassare.

REVIEW DIALOGUES

Ci sono cinque dialoghi di revisione alla fine del corso. I dialoghi ti aiuteranno a imparare l'inglese informale. Ogni dialogo ha domande per testare la tua comprensione. Non dimenticarti di utilizzare il dizionario se hai bisogno di aiuto con qualsiasi nuovo vocabolo.

PROGRESS BAR

La barra di avanzamento ti dice a che punto sei del corso.

AUDIO

Cerca questo simbolo ⓟ in ogni lezione, ti dirà quale traccia audio ascoltare per ogni sezione che ha un audio. Se non vedi il simbolo significa che non c'è alcun audio per quella sezione.

GRAMMAR SUMMARY

Alla fine del libro troverai una sintesi di grammatica che copre tutte le nozioni incluse in *Essential English*.

FREE ONLINE TOOLS

Vai a **www.livinglanguage.com/languagelab** e troverai tanti strumenti totalmente gratuiti. Ci sono flashcard con immagini e audio, e anche giochi interattivi.

Lesson 1:
Hello! How Are You?

Hello! In this lesson, you'll learn some basic expressions and other useful words and phrases to get you started speaking English. You'll learn how to:

☐ say **hello** and **my name is ...**

☐ ask **how are you?** and say **I'm fine**

☐ talk about where people are **from**

☐ say **I am**, **you are**, **she is**, and so on ...

☐ put it all together in a simple conversation

If you see ▶ listen as you read the book. Let's begin!

Hello! How Are You?   Big or Small? Short or Tall?   Everyday Life

This Is My Family   Welcome to My Home!

Vocabulary Builder 1

▶ 1A Vocabulary Builder 1 (CD 1, Track 2)

Write the translation of the word(s) on the left in the empty box on the right.

Hi!	
Hello!	
Good morning!	
How are you?	
I'm fine, thanks!	
What's your name?	
My name is John.	
Where are you from?	
I'm from Boston.	
What do you do, John?	
I'm a student at the university.	
Nice to meet you!	
Good-bye!	

✎ Vocabulary Practice 1

▶ 1B Vocabulary Practice 1 (CD 1, Track 3)

Let's practice the vocabulary you've learned. Listen and fill in the blanks.

1. _____!

2. _____!

3. Good_____!

4. How_____ you?

5. I'm_____, thanks.

6. _____ your name?

7. _____ name is John.

8. _____ are you _____ ?

9. _____ from Boston.

10. I'm a_____ at the _____ .

11. Nice_____ meet you.

12. _____ .

ANSWER KEY

1. Hi! 2. Hello! 3. morning; 4. are; 5. fine; 6. What's; 7. My; 8. Where, from; 9. I'm; 10. student, university; 11. to; 12. Good-bye.

Grammar Builder 1

▶ 1C Grammar Builder 1 (CD 1, Track 4)

HELLO! HOW ARE YOU?

(At 9:30 a.m.)

Good morning, John!	
Hi, Mary. How are you?	
I'm fine, thanks. And you?	
I'm good.	

(At 2:00 p.m.)

Hello, Professor Ramirez.	
Good afternoon, Mary. How are you doing?	
Very well, thank you.	

Hello! How Are You?   Big or Small? Short or Tall?   Everyday Life

This Is My Family   Welcome to My Home!

(At 7:00 p.m.)

Good evening, Mr. Johnson.	
Good evening, Mrs. Chang. It's so nice to see you.	

(At 11:00 p.m.)

Good-bye, John.	
Good night, Mary.	

Take it Further

▶ 1D Take It Further (CD 1, Track 5)

If someone asks **how are you?** You can answer:

	I'm great! I'm fantastic! I'm really good! or **I'm fine. I'm good.**
	I'm okay. or **So-so.**
	Not well. Not good.

A friendly, casual way to ask **how are you?** is **how's it going?** You can answer:

	Great! Fantastic! Really well! or **Fine. Well.**
	Okay. or **So-so.**
	Not well.

Vocabulary Builder 2

▶ 1E Vocabulary Builder 2 (CD 1, Track 6)

This is John.	
John is from Boston, in the United States.	
He is American.	
This is Hiroko.	
Hiroko is from Tokyo, in Japan.	
She is Japanese.	
This is Diego.	
Diego is from Guadalajara, in Mexico.	
He is Mexican.	

Hello! How Are You?   Big or Small? Short or Tall?   Everyday Life

This Is My Family   Welcome to My Home!

This is Li.	
Li is from Beijing, in China.	
Li is Chinese.	
This is Ahmed.	
Ahmed is from Cairo, in Egypt.	
He is Egyptian.	
This is Martine.	
Martine is from Paris, in France.	
Martine is French.	

✎ Vocabulary Practice 2

Give the nationalities.

1. John is from Boston, so he's _____.

2. Hiroko is from Tokyo, so she's _____.

3. Li is from Beijing, so he's _____.

4. Diego is from Guadalajara, so he's _____.

5. Ahmed is from Cairo, so he's _____.

6. Martine is from Paris, so she's _____.

ANSWER KEY
1. American; 2. Japanese; 3. Chinese; 4. Mexican; 5. Egyptian; 6. French

Now give the countries.

1. Beijing is in _____.

2. Cairo is in _____.

3. Boston is in _____.

4. Paris is in _____.

5. Guadalajara is in _____.

6. Tokyo is in _____.

ANSWER KEY

1. China; 2. Egypt; 3. the United States; 4. France; 5. Mexico; 6. Japan

Grammar Builder 2

▷ 1F Grammar Builder 2 (CD 1, Track 7)

THE VERB TO BE

I am (I'm)	we are (we're)
you are (you're)	you are (you're)
he is, she is, it is (he's, she's, it's)	they are (they're)

Now let's look at some examples.

I'm John. I'm a student. I'm from Boston.	
You're Hiroko, and you're from Japan.	
This is Diego. He's from Mexico.	
We're Martine and François. We're French.	
Ahmed and Layla, you're from Cairo.	
Li and Ming are from Beijing. They're Chinese.	

Hello! How Are You?　　　Big or Small? Short or Tall?　　　Everyday Life

This Is My Family　　　Welcome to My Home!

✎ Work Out 1

▶ 1G Work Out 1 (CD 1, Track 8)

Listen and write the words you hear.

1. Diego _____ from Guadalajara.

2. Maria _____ from Guadalajara, too.

3. Martine and François _____ French.

4. John _____ a student.

5. Where _____ you from?

6. I _____ from New York.

7. She _____ from Delhi.

8. How _____ they doing?

9. Ahmed _____ in Cairo.

10. Ahmed and Layla _____ in Cairo.

ANSWER KEY
1. is; 2. is; 3. are; 4. is; 5. are; 6. am; 7. is; 8. are; 9. is; 10. are

❝ Bring It All Together

▶ 1H Bring It All Together (CD 1, Track 9)

Now let's bring it all together, and add a little bit more vocabulary and structure. John is a student at a university in Boston. He's at a party, the day before classes start. Listen as he introduces himself to Mary.

John:　　　Hi.

Mary:　　　Oh, hi there.

John:　　　I'm John. What's your name?

Mary:	Hi, John. I'm Mary. Nice to meet you.
John:	Nice to meet you, too. So, Mary, how's it going?
Mary:	Fine, thanks.
Mary:	This is a good party.
John:	Yeah. Are you a student here at the university?
Mary:	No, I'm not a student.
John:	What do you do?
Mary:	I'm a professor.
John:	Oh … A professor of what?
Mary:	American literature.
John:	Hmm … I have a class tomorrow. American literature of the …
Mary:	… Twentieth Century?
John:	Yes, that's the one.
Mary:	Well, John, I'll see you in class tomorrow!
John:	Oh, right. Well, um, good night …
Mary:	… Professor Wheaton. Good night, John. Very nice to meet you!

✎ Work Out 2

Fill in the blanks with the correct word from the list below.

student, meet, are, I'm, your, university, name, nice, thanks

Bill:	Hi. My (1) _____ is Bill. What's (2) _____ name?
Peter:	I'm Peter.
Bill:	How (3) _____ you, Peter?
Peter:	I'm fine, (4)_____ . And you?
Bill:	I'm good.
Peter:	Are you a (5) _____ at the (6) _____ ?

Hello! How Are You?   Big or Small? Short or Tall?   Everyday Life

This Is My Family   Welcome to My Home!

Bill: Yes. And you?

Peter: (7)_____ a student here, too.

Bill: (8) _____ to meet you, Peter.

Peter: Nice to (9) _____ you, too.

ANSWER KEY

1. name; 2. your; 3. are; 4. thanks; 5. student; 6. university; 7. I'm; 8. Nice; 9. meet

Choose the best word.

1. John _____ from Boston

   a. am

   b. are

   c. is

   d. be

2. Marie is from Paris. _____ is French

   a. He

   b. She

   c. I

   d. You

3. Diego and Maria _____ from Mexico.

   a. he

   b. is

   c. they

   d. are

4. _____ are Mexican.

   a. **I**

   b. **They**

   c. **He**

   d. **She**

5. I_____ a student at the university.

   a. **am**

   b. **is**

   c. **be**

   d. **are**

6. It's_____ to meet you, Mrs. Chang.

   a. **here**

   b. **fine**

   c. **nice**

   d. **so-so**

ANSWER KEY
1. c; 2. b; 3. d; 4. b; 5. a; 6. c

✎ Drive It Home

Let's practice more! Follow the example:

example: John, the United States.
answer: John **is from** the United States. **He is** American.

Hello! How Are You?   Big or Small? Short or Tall?   Everyday Life

This Is My Family   Welcome to My Home!

1. Hiroko, Japan

_____

2. Ahmed, Egypt

_____

3. Diego, Mexico

_____

4. Martine, France

_____

5. Li, China

_____

ANSWER KEY

1. Hiroko is from Japan. She is Japanese. 2. Ahmed is from Egypt. He is Egyptian. 3. Diego is from Mexico. He is Mexican. 4. Martine is from France. She is French. 5. Li is from China. He is Chinese.

Take it Further

▶ 1I Take It Further (CD 1, Track 10)

Here are some countries, nationalities, and languages:

People from Mexico are Mexican, and they speak Spanish.	
People from China are Chinese, and they speak Mandarin and other languages.	
People from India are Indian, and they speak Hindi and other languages.	

People from Canada are Canadian, and they speak English and French.	
People from Japan are Japanese, and they speak Japanese.	
People from Egypt are Egyptian, and they speak Arabic.	
People from Russia are Russian, and they speak Russian.	
People from the United Kingdom are British, and they speak English.	
People from France are French, and they speak French.	
People from Brazil are Brazilian, and they speak Portuguese.	
People from Korea are Korean, and they speak Korean.	

What country are you from?

What language do you speak?

Hello! How Are You?   Big or Small? Short or Tall?   Everyday Life

This Is My Family   Welcome to My Home!

Parting Words

Well done! You just finished your first lesson of English. Can you:

☐ say **hello** and **my name is ... ?** (No? Go to page 44.)

☐ ask **how are you?** and say **I'm fine?** (No? Go to page 45.)

☐ talk about where people are **from?** (No? Go to page 47.)

☐ say **I am, you are, she is,** and so on ... ? (No? Go to page 49.)

☐ put it all together in a simple conversation? (No? Go to page 50.)

Don't forget to practice and reinforce what you've learned by visiting www.livinglanguage.com/languagelab for flashcards, games, and quizzes!

Word Recall

Do you remember these words from Lesson 1? Fill in the blanks.

1. _____ morning!

2. _____ are you?

3. _____ fine, thanks!

4. _____ your name?

5. Where are you_____ ?

6. I'm a_____ at the university.

7. _____ is Hiroko.

8. Hiroko_____ from Tokyo, in Japan.

9. _____ is Japanese.

10. This_____ Diego.

11. Diego is from Guadalajara,_____ Mexico.

12. _____ is Mexican.

ANSWER KEY
1. Good; 2. How; 3. I'm; 4. What's; 5. from; 6. student; 7. This; 8. is; 9. She; 10. is; 11. in; 12. He

Hello! How Are You?   Big or Small? Short or Tall?   Everyday Life

This Is My Family   Welcome to My Home!

Lesson 2:
This Is My Family

Hello again! In this lesson, we'll talk about people and the family. So you'll learn:

☐ basic vocabulary for **people** and the **family**

☐ how to use the verb **to have**

☐ more vocabulary for the **family**

☐ how to use **my, your, his, her, John's,** etc.

☐ how to put it all together in a conversation about a family photo

So let's get started with some simple greetings. Ready?

Vocabulary Builder 1

2A Vocabulary Builder 1 (CD 1, Track 11)

This is Paul Archer.	
He is a man.	
This is Laura Archer.	
She is a woman.	
This is Jenny Archer.	
She is a girl.	
This is Billy Archer.	
He is a boy.	
This is the Archer family.	
Paul Archer is the father.	
Laura Archer is the mother.	
Jenny Archer is the daughter.	
And Billy Archer is the son.	

✎ Vocabulary Practice 1

Fill in the blanks.

1. Laura Archer is a _____.

2. In the Archer family, she is the _____.

3. Billy is a _____.

4. In the Archer family, he is the _____.

5. Jenny is a _____.

6. In the Archer family, she is the _____.

Hello! How Are You?   Big or Small? Short or Tall?   Everyday Life

This Is My Family   Welcome to My Home!

7. Paul Archer is a _____ .

8. In the Archer family, he is the _____ .

ANSWER KEY
1. woman; 2. mother; 3. boy; 4. son; 5. girl; 6. daughter; 7. man; 8. father

Grammar Builder 1
▶ 2B Grammar Builder 1 (CD 1, Track 12)

THE VERB TO HAVE

In Lesson 1 you saw the important verb to be. Now let's see another important verb, to have.

I have	we have
you have	you have
he has, she has, it has	they have

Let's take a look at some examples.

Paul Archer has a wife, Laura Archer.	
Laura Archer has a husband, Paul Archer.	
Paul and Laura Archer have children.	
They have a daughter, Jenny.	
They also have a son, Billy.	
Jenny has a brother, Billy.	
And Billy has a sister, Jenny.	
They have parents, a mother and a father.	

Take it Further

▶ 2C Take It Further (CD 1, Track 13)

Now you know mother, father, daughter, and son. But parents have parents, too!

Paul Archer's father is Tom Archer.	
Tom Archer is Billy and Jenny's grandfather.	
Paul Archer's mother is Betty Archer.	
Betty Archer is Billy and Jenny's grandmother.	
Tom and Betty Archer are Billy and Jenny's grandparents.	
Jenny is Tom and Betty's granddaughter.	
Billy is Tom and Betty's grandson.	
Jenny and Billy are Tom and Betty's grandchildren.	

Vocabulary Builder 2

▶ 2D Vocabulary Builder 2 (CD 1, Track 14)

Laura Archer's brother is Brian Smith.	
Brian has a wife, Sarah Smith.	
Brian and Sarah have a son, Max.	
Brian Smith is Billy and Jenny's uncle.	

Hello! How Are You?   Big or Small? Short or Tall?   Everyday Life

This Is My Family   Welcome to My Home!

Sarah Smith is Billy and Jenny's aunt.	
Max is Billy and Jenny's cousin.	
Billy is Brian and Sarah's nephew.	
Jenny is Brian and Sarah's niece.	

✎ Vocabulary Practice 2

▶ 2E Vocabulary Practice 2 (CD 1, Track 15)

Let's practice the vocabulary you've learned. Listen again, and fill in the blanks.

1. Laura Archer's _____ is Brian Smith.

2. Brian has a _____, Sarah Smith.

3. Brian and Sarah have a _____, Max.

4. Brian Smith is Billy and Jenny's _____.

5. Sarah Smith is Billy and Jenny's _____.

6. Max is Billy and Jenny's _____.

7. Billy is Brian and Sarah's _____.

8. Jenny is Brian and Sarah's _____.

ANSWER KEY
1. brother; 2. wife; 3. son; 4. uncle; 5. aunt; 6. cousin; 7. nephew; 8. niece

Grammar Builder 2

▶ 2F Grammar Builder 2 (CD 1, Track 16)

MY, YOUR, HIS ...

You learned the verb **to have** in Grammar Builder 1. Now let's look at other ways to talk about what you have.

my	our
your	your
his, her, its	their

Here are some examples:

I have a brother. My brother is Billy.	
You have a sister. Your sister is Jenny.	
She has a cousin. Her cousin is Max.	
He has a cousin, too. His cousin is Max.	
We have a son. Our son is Billy.	
They have a daughter. Their daughter is Jenny.	

You also saw **'s**, as in:

Laura Archer's brother is Brian Smith. = Her brother is Brian Smith.
Max is Billy and Jenny's cousin. = Max is their cousin.

✎ Work Out 1

▶ 2G Work Out 1 (CD 1, Track 17)

Listen and write the words you hear.

Hello! How Are You?   Big or Small? Short or Tall?   Everyday Life

This Is My Family   Welcome to My Home!

1. This is my cousin. _____ name is Jack.

2. Jack _____ a sister. _____ name is Anne.

3. Jack and _____ mother is a professor.

4. _____ father is a professor, too.

5. They _____ a cousin.

6. _____ cousin's name is Gary.

7. _____ name is Chris.

8. What's _____ name?

ANSWER KEY
1. **His**; 2. **has, Her**; 3. **Anne's**; 4. **Their**; 5. **have**; 6. **Their**; 7. **My**; 8. **your**

Bring It All Together

▶ 2H Bring It All Together (CD 1, Track 18)

Listen as Jenny shows Greg a photo of her family.

Greg:	Is this your family in the photo?
Jenny:	Yes.
Greg:	Who is this man?
Jenny:	That's my father. He's a professor at the university.
Greg:	And is that your mother?
Jenny:	Yes, that's my mother. She's a professor, too.
Greg:	You have two brothers?
Jenny:	No, I have one brother. This is my brother. His name is Joe.
Greg:	And who is the other boy?
Jenny:	He's my cousin, Michael.
Greg:	And these are your grandparents?
Jenny:	Yes, this is my grandmother, and this is my grandfather.

Greg: Where are they from?

Jenny: They're from Chicago.

Take It Further

▶ 2I Take It Further (CD 1, Track 19)

Greg asked, **you have two brothers?** Notice the −s on the plural (two or more).

one brother	two brothers
one sister	two sisters
one boy	two boys
one girl	two girls

Some plurals are irregular.

one man	two men
one woman	two women
one child	two children

We'll see more plurals in Lesson 3.

✎ Work Out 2

Write **have** or **has**.

1. I _____ two sisters.

2. My sister _____ a brother.

3. The boys _____ two cousins.

4. We _____ two grandmothers and two grandfathers.

5. My grandparents _____ six grandchildren.

Hello! How Are You?   Big or Small? Short or Tall?   Everyday Life

This Is My Family   Welcome to My Home!

6. Billy _____ a sister.

7. Mr. and Mrs. Archer _____ two children, a son and a daughter.

8. You _____ a brother and two sisters.

9. My mother _____ a husband.

10. And my father _____ a wife.

ANSWER KEY
1. have; 2. has; 3. have; 4. have; 5. have; 6. has; 7. have; 8. have; 9. has; 10; has

Now write **my, your, his, her, our,** or **their.**

1. You have a cousin. _____ cousin's name is Max.

2. I have two sisters. _____ names are Silvia and Maria.

3. We have a mother and a father. _____ names are Sue and Albert.

4. My uncle has a son. _____ name is Jeff.

5. My aunt has a daughter. _____ name is Teresa.

6. We have two children. _____ children's names are Billy and Jenny.

7. I have a sister. _____ sister's name is Jenny.

ANSWER KEY
1. Your; 2. Their; 3. Their; 4. His; 5. Her; 6. Our; 7. My

✎ Drive It Home

Let's talk about the Archer family. Remember Paul and Laura Archer, and their children Jenny and Billy? Don't forget the grandparents, Tom and Betty Archer, or Laura's brother Brian Smith, his wife, Sarah Smith, and their son, Max Smith. Now, write the family terms.

I am Jenny Archer.

1. Paul Archer is my_____.

2. Laura Archer is his_____, and my _____.

3. Billy is my_____, and I am his _____.

4. Max is our_____.

5. His_____ are Brian and Sarah Smith.

6. Brian Smith is my_____, and I am his _____.

7. Sarah Smith is my_____, and my brother Billy is her _____.

8. Tom Archer is my_____, and Betty Archer is my

_____.

ANSWER KEY

1. father; 2. wife, mother; 3. brother, sister; 4. cousin; 5. parents; 6. uncle, niece; 7. aunt, nephew;
8. grandfather, grandmother

Hello! How Are You?   Big or Small? Short or Tall?   Everyday Life

This Is My Family   Welcome to My Home!

Parting Words

Great! You finished the lesson on the family. Now you know:

- ☐ basic vocabulary for **people** and the **family** (No? Go to page 59.)

- ☐ how to use the verb **to have** (No? Go to page 60.)

- ☐ more vocabulary for the **family** (No? Go to page 61.)

- ☐ how to use **my**, **your**, **his**, **her**, **John's**, etc. (No? Go to page 63.)

- ☐ How to put it all together in a conversation about a family photo (No? Go to page 64.)

Don't forget to practice and reinforce what you've learned by visiting www.livinglanguage.com/languagelab for flashcards, games, and quizzes!

Word Recall

Let's practice the family vocabulary from Lesson 2.

1. My brother's father is my _____.

2. My mother's daughter is my _____.

3. My mother's son is my _____.

4. My father's wife is my _____.

5. My mother's brother is my _____.

6. And my mother's sister is my _____.

7. My aunt and uncle's daughter is my _____.

8. I'm a girl; I am my father and mother's _____.

9. I'm a girl; I am my aunt and uncle's _____.

10. I'm a boy; I am my father and mother's _____.

11. I'm a boy; I am my aunt and uncle's _____.

12. My father's mother is my _____.

13. And my father's father is my _____.

14. My grandmother and grandfather are my _____.

ANSWER KEY
1. father; 2. sister; 3. brother; 4. mother; 5. uncle; 6. aunt; 7. cousin; 8. daughter; 9. niece; 10. son;
11. nephew; 12. grandmother; 13. grandfather; 14. grandparents

Hello! How Are You?   Big or Small? Short or Tall?   Everyday Life

          This Is My Family   Welcome to My Home!

Lesson 3:
Big or Small? Short or Tall?

Welcome to Lesson 3! In this lesson, we'll talk about adjectives like big, small, short, and tall. We'll also review numbers. So you'll learn:

☐ how to describe things with words like big, small, beautiful, and ugly

☐ how to ask yes/no questions with be and have

☐ how to use there is and there are

☐ how to use numbers and the plural

☐ how to put it all together in a simple conversation about John's class

Let's begin!

Vocabulary Builder 1

▶ 3A Vocabulary Builder 1 (CD 1, Track 20)

Canada is a big country.	
Singapore is a small country.	
Paris is a beautiful city.	
Paris is not an ugly city.	
The Sahara is very hot.	
Antarctica is very cold.	
The Amazon is a long river.	
The Amazon is not short.	
I am in New York; Philadelphia is near.	
I am in New York; Beijing is far.	
Mr. Archer is a man; he is tall.	
Billy is a boy; he is short.	
Billy's grandfather is old.	
Billy is not old, he's young.	
My professor is excellent; she is very good.	
Your professor is not good; he's bad!	
1+1 is easy.	
$2x(3y-4x)=2y/x$ is hard!	

✎ Vocabulary Practice 1

Let's practice the vocabulary you've learned.

1. China is not a small country; it's a _____ country.

Hello! How Are You?   Big or Small? Short or Tall?   Everyday Life

This Is My Family   Welcome to My Home!

2. The Amazon is not a short river; it's a _____ river.

3. My grandparents are not young; they are _____.

4. Antarctica is very _____.

5. Saudi Arabia is not cold; it's _____.

6. You're in Philadelphia, so New York is _____.

7. You're in Philadelphia, so Tokyo is _____.

8. My professor is not bad; he's very _____.

9. The woman is not _____; she's tall.

10. San Francisco is not an ugly city; it's a _____ city.

11. What's one plus one? That's an _____ question!

12. But the professor's question isn't easy; it's _____.

ANSWER KEY
1. big; 2. long; 3. old; 4. cold; 5. hot; 6. near; 7. far; 8. good; 9. short; 10. beautiful; 11. easy; 12. hard

Take It Further
▶ 3B Take It Further (CD 1, Track 21)

Colors are useful adjectives.

The sky at night is black.	
Snow is white.	
Roses are red.	
The ocean is blue.	
Plants are green.	
Bananas are yellow.	
Tea is brown.	

| Let's Eat! | At Work | Review Dialogues |

Around Town | Let's Go Shopping | What Do You Feel Like Doing?

Oranges are orange.	
Grapes are purple.	
Elephants are gray.	

Let's look at some more example sentences.

The American flag is red, white, and blue.	
The Chinese flag is red and yellow.	
The Indian flag is orange, green, white, and blue.	
At night, the sky is black, but during the day, the sky is blue.	

Grammar Builder 1

▶ 3C Grammar Builder 1 (CD 1, Track 22)

YES **OR** NO?

To ask a question with **am**, **is**, or **are**, move the verb to the front.

I am . . .	Am I . . . ?
You are a professor.	Are you a professor?
He is Chinese.	Is he Chinese?
Martine is French.	Is Martine French?
We are at the university.	Are we at the university?
The children are young.	Are the children young?

To answer a **be** question, use **yes** or **no** + **not**.

Hello! How Are You?   Big or Small? Short or Tall?   Everyday Life

This Is My Family   Welcome to My Home!

Is New York a beautiful city?

Yes, New York is a beautiful city.

or

No, New York is not a beautiful city.

Is he a good professor?

Yes, he is a good professor.

or

No, he is not a good professor.

Is Chicago far?

Yes, Chicago is far.

or

No, Chicago is not far.

To ask a question with **have**, use **do … have?**

I have …	Do I have … ?
You have a sister.	Do you have a sister?
They have children.	Do they have children?

To ask a question with **has**, use **does … have?**

He has …	Does he have … ?
She has …	Does she have … ?
Jenny has a brother.	Does Jenny have a brother?
Billy has a sister.	Does Billy have a sister?

To answer a **have** question, use **yes** or **no + do not have.**

Do they have children?

Yes, they have children.

or

No, they do not have children.

Do we have a good professor?

Yes, we have a good professor.

or

No, we do not have a good professor.

To answer a **has** question, use **yes** or **no** + **does not have.**

Does Bob have a wife?

Yes, he has a wife.

or

No, he does not have a wife.

Does Mrs. Archer have children?

Yes, she has children.

or

No, she does not have children.

Take it Further

▶ 3D Take It Further (CD 1, Track 23)

In Lesson 1 you learned both long forms of **be** (**I am, you are, he is, we are, they are**) and short forms (**I'm, you're, she's, we're, they're**). The short forms are **contractions.** There are also contractions with **not.** Let's look at **be** first.

Am I a professor?	No, I'm not a professor.
Are you a student?	No, you're not a student.
	No, you aren't a student.

Hello! How Are You?   Big or Small? Short or Tall?   Everyday Life

This Is My Family   Welcome to My Home!

Is he a student?	No he's not a student.
	No he isn't a student.
Are we in Boston?	No, we're not in Boston.
	No, we aren't in Boston.
Are they near?	No, they're not near.
	No, they aren't near.

With I, there is one contraction (I'm not). But with you, he, she, it, we, and they, there are two: pronoun + be (I'm, you're, etc.) and be + not (aren't, isn't, etc.).

PRONOUN + BE	BE + NOT
I'm not	—
you're not	you aren't
he's not	he isn't
she's not	she isn't
it's not	it isn't
we're not	we aren't
they're not	they aren't

With have, there are only do/does + not contractions.

Do I have children?	No, I don't have children.
Do you have a son?	No, you don't have a son.
Does he have a good professor?	No, he doesn't have a good professor.
Does she have a brother?	No, she doesn't have a brother.
Do we have cousins?	No, we don't have cousins.
Do they have a daughter?	No, they don't have a daughter.

Vocabulary Builder 2

▶ 3E Vocabulary Builder 2 (CD 1, Track 24)

There is a good university in the city.	
There are two good universities in the city.	
There is an excellent professor at the university.	
There are excellent professors at the university.	
There is a young girl in the family.	
There are three young girls in the family.	
There are tall buildings in New York.	
There are long rivers in South America.	
There is excellent wine from France.	
There are beautiful cities in Europe.	

✎ Vocabulary Practice 2

▶ 3F Vocabulary Practice 2 (CD 1, Track 25)

Listen again, and write the words that you hear.

1. _____ is a good university in the city.

2. There _____ two good universities in the city.

3. There _____ an excellent professor at the university.

4. _____ excellent professors at the university.

Hello! How Are You?   Big or Small? Short or Tall?   Everyday Life

This Is My Family   Welcome to My Home!

5. _____ a young girl in the family.

6. There are three young _____ in the family.

7. There are tall _____ in New York.

8. There are _____ rivers in South America.

9. _____ excellent wine from France.

10. There are beautiful _____ in Europe.

ANSWER KEY
1. There; 2. are; 3. is; 4. There are; 5. There is; 6. girls; 7. buildings; 8. long; 9. There is; 10. cities

Grammar Builder 2

▶ 3G Grammar Builder 2 (CD 1, Track 26)

NUMBERS AND PLURALS

Let's review the numbers in English.

one, two, three	1, 2, 3
four, five, six	4, 5, 6
seven, eight	7, 8
nine, ten	9, 10

Most of the numbers from 11 to 19 end in –teen.

eleven, twelve, thirteen	11, 12, 13
fourteen, fifteen, sixteen	14, 15, 16
seventeen, eighteen, nineteen	17, 18, 19

The tens from 20 to 90 end in –ty

twenty, thirty, forty	20, 30, 40
fifty, sixty, seventy	50, 60, 70

| eighty, ninety, one hundred | 80, 90, 100 |

To say 21, 32, 43, and so on, just put the two numbers together.

twenty-one, twenty-two, twenty-three	21, 22, 23
thirty-four, thirty-five, thirty-six	34, 35, 36
forty-seven, fifty-eight, ninety-nine	47, 58, 99

To give an age, use a form of be and a number, or be + years old. The question is how old is/are … ?

How old is Billy?	He's ten years old.
How old is Jenny?	She's fourteen.
How old is Billy and Jenny's grandmother?	She's sixty-three.
How old are Billy and Jenny?	They are ten and fourteen years old.

With one, use the singular. With two or more, use the plural. Most nouns add –s in the plural.

one boy	two boys, three boys
one student	ten students, fifteen students
one professor	five professors, twenty professors

If a noun ends in –y, the plural ends in –ies.

one university	two universities
one country	three countries
one city	four cities

Some nouns have irregular plurals.

| one man | two men |
| one woman | three women |

Hello! How Are You?   Big or Small? Short or Tall?   Everyday Life

This Is My Family   Welcome to My Home!

one child	four children
one person	ten people

With the singular, use **there is** (**there's**). With the plural, use **there are**.

There is ...	There are ...
There is a good university in the city.	There are three good universities in the city.
There is a very good student in the class.	There are very good students in the class.
There is one boy in the family.	There are three boys in the family.

✎ Work Out 1

▶ 3H Work Out 1 (CD 1, Track 27)

Listen and write the words you hear.

1. Billy is a _____ boy. He is _____ years old.

2. He _____ a big family, he has a _____ family.

3. _____ four people in his family.

4. Billy's father's _____ is Paul.

5. _____ mother's name is Laura.

6. Billy _____ have a brother, but he _____ a sister.

7. His _____ name is Jenny.

8. Jenny is _____ .

9. Billy and Jenny _____ a cousin.

10. His name is Max, and he is _____ .

ANSWER KEY

1. young, ten; 2. doesn't have, small; 3. There are; 4. name; 5. His; 6. doesn't, has; 7. sister's; 8. fourteen; 9. have; 10. nine years old

🔊 Bring It All Together

▶ 3I Bring It All Together (CD 1, Track 28)

You met John in Lesson 1. John is a student at the university. He has a class called American Literature of the Twentieth Century. But John is not a very good student. Listen in as he talks to his friend Diane.

Diane:	Are you in Professor Wheaton's class?
John:	Yes, I am. It's American Literature of the Twentieth Century.
Diane:	Is it a good class?
John:	Yes, it's very good, but it's hard!
Diane:	Is Professor Wheaton a good professor?
John:	Yes, she's very smart, but her questions are hard! And the books are hard!
Diane:	How many students are there in the class?
John:	There are twenty-three students in the class.
Diane:	Are there good students in the class?
John:	Yes, there are three or four excellent students in the class.
Diane:	Are you an excellent student?
John:	No, I'm not an excellent student.
Diane:	Well, are you a good student?
John:	No, I'm not a good student. I'm an okay student.
Diane:	An okay student? Do you have homework tonight?
John:	Yes, I have homework, but there's a party tonight, and …

Hello! How Are You?   Big or Small? Short or Tall?   Everyday Life

This Is My Family   Welcome to My Home!

Diane:	John! You have homework tonight!
John:	Yes, I do. But there's a party, and ...
Diane:	And you're not an excellent student!

Take It Further

▶ 3J Take it Further (CD 1, Track 29)

You learned about yes/no questions in this lesson. Other questions have question words. In Lessons 1, 2, and 3, you have seen:

What?
What's your name?
My name is John.

Who?
Who is this man?
He's my father.

How?
How are you?
I'm fine, thanks.

How old is Billy?
He's ten years old.

How many?
How many students are there in the class?
There are twenty-three students in the class.

✎ Work Out 2

Choose there is or there are.

1. _____ very good wine from France.

2. _____ fifty states in the United States.

3. _____ tall buildings in New York.

4. _____ an excellent student in the class.

5. _____ twenty-three students in the class.

6. _____ two girls in the family.

7. _____ a very long river in Brazil.

8. _____ three children in the family.

ANSWER KEY
1. There is; 2. There are; 3. There are; 4. There is; 5. There are; 6. There are; 7. There is; 8. There are

Choose the right word.

1. You (have/has) three sisters.

2. (Do/Does) she have a brother?

3. Yes, she (have/has) a brother.

4. No, she (doesn't/don't) have a brother.

5. The man (have/has) a wife.

6. The man doesn't (have/has) a wife.

7. I (don't/doesn't) have a sister.

8. We don't (have/has) a big family.

Hello! How Are You?   Big or Small? Short or Tall?   Everyday Life

This Is My Family   Welcome to My Home!

ANSWER KEY

1. have; 2. Does; 3. has; 4. doesn't; 5. has; 6. have; 7. don't; 8. have

Now, form questions. For example, you'll see: She has a sister. And you'll write: Does she have a sister?

1. He is tall.

   _____

2. The girls have a brother.

   _____

3. The family is big.

   _____

4. The professors are very good.

   _____

5. The students have an easy class.

   _____

6. The boy has a sister.

   _____

7. The river is long.

   _____

8. Canada and China are big countries.

   _____

ANSWER KEY

1. Is he tall? 2. Do the girls have a brother? 3. Is the family big? 4. Are the professors very good?
5. Do the students have an easy class? 6. Does the boy have a sister? 7. Is the river long?
8. Are Canada and China big countries?

| Let's Eat! | At Work | Review Dialogues |

Around Town · Let's Go Shopping · What Do You Feel Like Doing?

✎ Drive It Home

Let's practice questions and answers. First, with be.

Example: Is New York a beautiful city?
Yes, New York is a beautiful city.
No, New York is not a beautiful city.

1. Is it a big country? (Yes, it … , No, it …)

   _____

2. Is the professor good? (Yes, she … , No, she …)

   _____

3. Are the questions easy? (Yes, they … , No, they …)

   _____

4. Are the children very young? (Yes, they … , No, they …)

   _____

ANSWER KEY

1. Yes, it's a big country./No, it isn't/it's not a big country. 2. Yes, she's good./No, she isn't/she's not good. 3. Yes, they're easy./No, they aren't/they're not easy. 4. Yes, they're young./No, they're not/they aren't young.

Great. Now let's practice questions and answers with have.

Example: Do we have a good professor?
Yes, we have a good professor.
No, we don't have a good professor.

Hello! How Are You?   **Big or Small? Short or Tall?**   Everyday Life

This Is My Family   Welcome to My Home!

1. Does she have a brother? (**Yes, she …, No, she …**)

2. Do they have children? (**Yes, they …, No, they …**)

3. Does she have a husband? (**Yes, she …, No, she …**)

4. Do the boys have a sister? (**Yes, they …, No, they …**)

ANSWER KEY
1. Yes, she has a brother./No, she doesn't have a brother. 2. Yes, they have children./No, they don't have children. 3. Yes, she has a husband./No, she doesn't have a husband. 4. Yes, they have a sister./No, they don't have a sister.

Parting Words

Terrific! You just finished Lesson 3. Do you know:

☐ how to describe things with words like **big, small, beautiful,** and **ugly**? (No? Go back to 71.)

☐ how to ask **yes/no** questions with **be** and **have**? (No? Go back to 73.)

☐ how to use **there is** and **there are?** (No? Go back to 77.)

☐ how to use numbers and the plural? (No? Go back to 78.)

☐ how to put it all together in a simple conversation about John's class? (No? Go back to 81.)

Don't forget to practice and reinforce what you've learned by visiting www.livinglanguage.com/languagelab for flashcards, games, and quizzes!

Word Recall

Give the opposites.

1. Their class is not good, it's _____.

2. Monaco is not big, it's _____.

3. Paris is not ugly, it's _____.

4. Antarctica is not hot, it's _____.

5. Your city is not near, it's _____.

6. His sister is not short, she's _____.

7. Our question is not hard, it's _____.

8. The Mississippi River is not short, it's _____.

9. The Sahara is not cold, it's _____.

10. My family is not small, it's _____.

11. The boy is not old, he's _____.

12. His class is not easy, it's _____.

13. The city is not beautiful, it's _____.

14. My grandmother is not young, she's _____.

ANSWER KEY
1. bad; 2. small; 3. beautiful; 4. cold; 5. far; 6. tall; 7. easy; 8. long; 9. hot; 10. big; 11. young; 12. hard;
13. ugly; 14. old

Hello! How Are You?   Big or Small? Short or Tall?   Everyday Life

This Is My Family   Welcome to My Home!

Lesson 4:
Welcome to My Home!

How are you? In this lesson, you'll learn how to talk about your home. That means that you'll learn:

☐ the names of rooms in a house or apartment

☐ how to use **the** and **a/an**

☐ the names of objects in a house or apartment

☐ how to use prepositions like **in**, **on**, and **under**

☐ how to tell people about your home

Vocabulary Builder 1

▶ 4A Vocabulary Builder 1 (CD 1, Track 30)

Do you live in an apartment or a house?	
We live in a house.	
The house has four bedrooms.	
It also has a comfortable living room.	
It has a sunny kitchen.	
And it has a large dining room.	
There are also two bathrooms in the house.	
And there's a quiet study with a desk, a new computer, and books.	
The house also has a garage.	
And it has a big yard with grass, trees, and a garden.	
Our family has a dog and a cat.	
The dog is black, and the cat is white.	

✎ Vocabulary Practice 1

▶ 4B Vocabulary Practice 1 (CD 1, Track 31)

Listen, again, and write the words that you hear.

1. Do you live in an _____ or a _____ ?

2. We _____ in a house.

3. The house has four _____.

Hello! How Are You? Big or Small? Short or Tall? Everyday Life

This Is My Family Welcome to My Home!

4. It also has a comfortable _____ .

5. It has a sunny _____ .

6. And it has a large _____ .

7. There are _____ two _____ in the house.

8. And there's a quiet _____ with a _____ , a new computer, and books.

9. The house also has a _____ .

10. And it has a big _____ with grass, trees, and a flower _____ .

11. Our family has _____ and _____ .

12. The dog is _____ , and the cat is _____ .

ANSWER KEY
1. apartment, house; 2. live; 3. bedrooms; 4. living room; 5. kitchen; 6. dining room;
7. also, bathrooms; 8. study, desk; 9. garage; 10. yard, garden; 11. a dog, a cat; 12. black; white

Take It Further

▶ 4C Take It Further (CD 1, Track 32)

Let's look at the new vocabulary from Vocabulary Builder 1.

There are rooms in a house or apartment. You learned: bedroom, living room, kitchen, dining room, bathroom, and study. What do people do in the rooms in a house?

People sleep in a bedroom.	
People watch television in a living room.	
People cook in a kitchen.	
People eat in a dining room.	

People wash in a bathroom.	
People read or write in a study.	

You also learned some new adjectives: sunny, comfortable, large, quiet, and new.

Miami is a sunny city; London is not a sunny city.	
A good chair or bed is comfortable. A bad chair or bed is not comfortable.	
Large is big. Do you have a large family or a small family?	
A library is quiet. A big party is not quiet. A big party is loud.	
New is not old. New computers are good.	

⊕ Culture Note

The backyard is important to many Americans. In the backyard, people garden (grow flowers, plants, and vegetables), have barbecues (grill meat and vegetables and eat outside), and play games. People also take care of their lawn (an area of grass). Some Americans also have porches in front of their homes where they sit and relax.

Hello! How Are You? Big or Small? Short or Tall? Everyday Life

This Is My Family Welcome to My Home!

Grammar Builder 1

▶ 4D Grammar Builder 1 (CD 1, Track 33)

USING THE AND A/AN

In a conversation, when you talk about something for the first time, use **a**.
Then, use **the**.

We live in **a house**. **The house** has four bedrooms. **The house** is big.	
There's **a living room** in the house. **The living room** is comfortable. But **the living room** is small.	
There's **a dining room** in the house. **The dining room** is large. **The dining room** is sunny.	
There's **a study** in the house. **The study** is quiet. There are books and a desk in **the study**.	

Say **an** instead of **a** if the next word begins with **a**, **e**, **i**, **o**, or **u**. However, **the**
remains the same.

I live in **an apartment**. **The apartment** is very small.	
There is **an excellent professor** at the university. **The professor's** name is Mary Wheaton.	

Use a or an with indefinite, general or non-specific things.

There is a new restaurant near the university. (Good? Bad? Italian? French? Thai? …)	
There's a new computer in the study. (Sony? Dell? HP? …)	
A man is in the classroom. (A professor? A student? …)	

Use the with definite or specific things.

The new restaurant near the university is very good.	
The new computer in the study is a Sony.	
The man in the classroom is a new student.	

Use the with famous things that everyone knows, because they're specific and definite.

The Statue of Liberty is in New York.	
The Eiffel Tower is in Paris.	
The White House is in Washington, D.C.	
The Taj Mahal is in India.	
The Great Wall is in China.	

Hello! How Are You?   Big or Small? Short or Tall?   Everyday Life

This Is My Family   **Welcome to My Home!**

Vocabulary Builder 2

▶ 4E Vocabulary Builder 2 (CD 1, Track 34)

I live in a small apartment.	
In the living room there are two chairs, a couch, a bookshelf, and a television.	
The couch is old, but the television is new.	
I have a refrigerator, a stove, a dishwasher, and a sink in the kitchen.	
The dishwasher is old, but it's good.	
There is also a table with two chairs in the kitchen.	
The table is very small, but the chairs are comfortable.	
There is a bed, a dresser, and a desk in my bedroom.	
The dresser has my clothes in it.	
Of course there's a bathroom in my apartment.	
The bathroom is very, very small!	
The bathroom has a toilet and shower, but it doesn't have a bathtub.	

✎ Vocabulary Practice 2

Choose the best answer.

1. The couch is in the _____.

   a. bedroom

   b. dining room

   c. bathroom

   d. living room

2. The _____ is in the kitchen.

   a. couch

   b. sink

   c. toilet

   d. bed

3. The _____ is in the dining room.

   a. table

   b. toilet

   c. bed

   d. dresser

4. The _____ is in the study.

   a. toilet

   b. stove

   c. bookshelf

   d. bed

Hello! How Are You?   Big or Small? Short or Tall?   Everyday Life

This Is My Family   Welcome to My Home!

5. The stove is in the _____.

   a. kitchen

   b. bedroom

   c. bathroom

   d. dining room

6. There is a new _____ in the living room.

   a. shower

   b. refrigerator

   c. bed

   d. television

7. The dishwasher is in the _____.

   a. dining room

   b. kitchen

   c. bedroom

   d. bathroom

8. The _____ is in the bathroom.

   a. stove

   b. toilet

   c. couch

   d. bed

9. The _____ is in the bedroom.

   a. sink

   b. shower

   c. stove

   d. bed

10. The refrigerator is in the_____.

   a. living room

   b. dining room

   c. kitchen

   d. bedroom

11. The dresser is in the_____.

   a. bedroom

   b. kitchen

   c. dining room

   d. living room

12. The_____ is in the bathroom.

   a. stove

   b. couch

   c. television

   d. shower

ANSWER KEY
1. d; 2. b; 3. a; 4. c; 5. a; 6. d; 7. b; 8. b; 9. d; 10. c; 11. a; 12. d

Hello! How Are You?   Big or Small? Short or Tall?   Everyday Life

This Is My Family   Welcome to My Home!

Grammar Builder 2

▶ 4F Grammar Builder 2 (CD 1, Track 35)

PREPOSITIONS: IN, ON, UNDER, ETC.

Let's look at how to use common prepositions.

IN

We live in a house.	
Beijing is in China.	

ON

The books are on the bookshelf.	
The computer is on the desk.	

FROM

Ram is from India.	
John is from Boston.	

NEXT TO

The chair is next to the table.	
New York is next to New Jersey.	

NEAR

New York is near Philadelphia.	
The restaurant is near the university.	

FAR FROM

Los Angeles is far from New York.	
South Africa is far from Japan.	

UNDER

The cat is under the couch.	
The dog is under the table.	

BETWEEN

The bathroom is between the bedroom and the kitchen.	
New York is between Boston and Philadelphia.	

✏ Work Out 1

▶ 4G Work Out 1 (CD 1, Track 36)

Listen and write the words you hear.

1. There's _____ under the bed.

2. _____ cat's name is Patches.

3. There is _____ very good student in the class.

4. _____ is from Chicago.

5. There is _____ excellent Thai restaurant _____ here.

6. _____ restaurant is _____ the university.

7. John has _____computer.

Hello! How Are You?   Big or Small? Short or Tall?   Everyday Life

This Is My Family   Welcome to My Home!

8. _____ computer is _____ his desk.

9. They _____ in _____ apartment.

10. _____ is small, but comfortable.

ANSWER KEY
1. a cat; 2. The; 3. a; 4. The student; 5. an, near; 6. The, next to; 7. a new; 8. The, on; 9. live, an;
10. The apartment

ⓖ Bring It All Together

▶ 4H Bring It All Together (CD 1, Track 37)

Sarah has a new apartment. Her friend Bill is visiting for the first time.

Bill:	Hey, Sarah! So, this is your new apartment?
Sarah:	Yes! Welcome to my new home!
Bill:	It's great. It's next to the university, and near really good restaurants.
Sarah:	Yeah, it's fantastic. This is my living room.
Bill:	It's very sunny. And is that a new couch?
Sarah:	Yes, the couch is new. The chair is old, though.
Bill:	But it's a comfortable chair.
Sarah:	Perfect for a good book.
Bill:	Or good television!
Sarah:	Yeah, that, too.
Bill:	How many bedrooms do you have?
Sarah:	There are two bedrooms. One is my bedroom, and the other is my study. I have a desk and bookshelves in there.
Bill:	Where's your computer?
Sarah:	The computer is in the study.
Bill:	And that's your kitchen?
Sarah:	Yeah, it's small and not very sunny. The refrigerator and stove are really old. And I don't have a dishwasher.

Bill:	No problem! You've got great restaurants right here! And … the bathroom?
Sarah:	It's very nice.
Bill:	No, where's the bathroom?
Sarah:	Oh! Right there, next to the bedroom.
Bill:	Thanks. I'll be right back …

✎ Work Out 2

Write **the**, **a**, or **an**.

1. Mr. Archer is _____ man.

2. Jenny is _____ excellent student.

3. John has _____ dog. _____ dog's name is Lola.

4. _____ Taj Mahal is in India.

5. There is _____ really good restaurant near here.

6. I have _____ new computer. _____ computer is really good.

7. Do you have _____ brother?

8. Where is _____ Grand Canyon?

9. Sarah has _____ apartment. _____ apartment is small, but comfortable.

10. There's _____ desk in the study.

11. Are you taking _____ English literature class?

12. Yes, I'm taking _____ English literature class. _____ professor is excellent.

ANSWER KEY
1. a; 2. an; 3. a, The; 4. The; 5. a; 6. a; The; 7. a; 8. the; 9. an, The; 10. a; 11. an; 12. an, The

Hello! How Are You?   Big or Small? Short or Tall?   Everyday Life

This Is My Family   Welcome to My Home!

Now choose the right preposition.

1. John is (**in/on**) his bedroom.

2. There is a book (**on/between**) the desk.

3. The bathroom is (**from/next to**) the bedroom.

4. Cape Town is (**near/far from**) Tokyo.

5. The dog is (**under/in**) the table.

6. Billy is (**from/between**) his mother and his father.

7. Yukiko is (**from/on**) Osaka.

8. London is (**on/in**) the United Kingdom.

9. There is a good Thai restaurant (**near/under**) the university.

10. There are twenty students (**in/from**) the class.

ANSWER KEY
1. in; 2. on; 3. next to; 4. far from; 5. under; 6. between; 7. from; 8. in; 9. near; 10. in

✎ Drive It Home

Let's practice **the**, **a**, and **an**. First, fill in these sentences with **a** or **an**.

1. There is _____ new student in the class.

2. There is _____ excellent restaurant near the university.

3. There is _____ good book on my desk.

4. There is _____ dining room in the house.

ANSWER KEY
1. a; 2. an; 3. a; 4. a

Now, continue the sentences with **the**.

1. There is a new student in the class. _____ student is from Chicago.

2. There is an excellent restaurant near the university. _____ restaurant is new.

3. There is a good book on my desk. _____ book is *War and Peace*.

4. There is a dining room in the house. _____ dining room is not very big.

ANSWER KEY
1. The; 2. The; 3. The; 4. The

Take It Further
▶ 4I Take It Further (CD 1, Track 38)

You know the numbers **one** through **one hundred**. Let's look at **first**, **second**, **third**, etc.

first, second, third, fourth	1st, 2nd, 3rd, 4th
fifth, sixth, seventh, eighth	5th, 6th, 7th, 8th
ninth, tenth, eleventh, twelfth	9th, 10th, 11th, 12th

Now let's look at some examples.

This is the fourth lesson of Essential English.	
January is the first month of the year.	
February is the second month of the year.	
Thursday is the fourth day of the work week.	

Hello! How Are You?   Big or Small? Short or Tall?   Everyday Life

This Is My Family   Welcome to My Home!

Parting Words

Well done! You just finished your fourth lesson of English. Do you know:

☐ the names of rooms in a house or apartment? (No? Go back to page 89.)

☐ how to use **the** and **a/an**? (No? Go back to page 92.)

☐ the names of objects in a house or apartment? (No? Go back to page 94.)

☐ how to use prepositions like **in**, **on**, and **under**? (No? Go back to page 98.)

☐ how to tell people about your home? (No? Go back to page 100.)

Don't forget to practice and reinforce what you've learned by visiting www.livinglanguage.com/languagelab for flashcards, games, and quizzes!

Word Recall

Do you remember these words?

1. What is not in the kitchen?

   a. the sink

   b. the refrigerator

   c. a bed

   d. a table

2. What is not in the living room?

   a. a television

   b. a couch

   c. a chair

   d. the shower

Hello! How Are You?   Big or Small? Short or Tall?   Everyday Life

This Is My Family   Welcome to My Home!

3. What is not in the bedroom?

   a. a sink

   b. a bed

   c. a dresser

   d. a chair

4. What is not in the bathroom?

   a. the toilet

   b. the stove

   c. the shower

   d. the sink

5. What is not in the study?

   a. a chair

   b. a desk

   c. the dishwasher

   d. the computer

ANSWER KEY
1. c; 2. d; 3. a; 4. b; 5. c

Lesson 5:
Everyday Life

In this lesson, we'll talk about everyday life. That means that you'll learn:

☐ the days of the week

☐ how to tell time

☐ common verbs for everyday life

☐ how to use verbs in the present tense

☐ how to put it all together in a short conversation about a typical day

So let's get started!

Hello! How Are You?　　　Big or Small? Short or Tall?　　　Everyday Life

This Is My Family　　　Welcome to My Home!

Vocabulary Builder 1

▶ 5A Vocabulary Builder 1 (CD 2, Track 1)

I wake up at seven o'clock in the morning.	
I brush my teeth and take a shower.	
I get dressed.	
I eat breakfast./I have breakfast.	
I read the newspaper.	
I go to work at eight thirty.	
I take the train to my office.	
I work from nine o'clock until six o'clock.	
I eat/have lunch at twelve thirty in the afternoon.	
I leave work at six o'clock in the evening.	
I get home at six thirty.	
I eat/have dinner with my family at seven o'clock.	
During dinner we talk about our day.	
After dinner we do the dishes and then watch television.	
The kids do their homework and listen to music.	
My wife and I read before bed.	
We go to sleep at eleven thirty at night.	

✎ Vocabulary Practice 1

▶ 5B Vocabulary Practice 1 (CD 2, Track 2)

Let's practice the vocabulary you've learned. Listen to the audio one more time and fill in the verbs that you hear.

1. I _____ up at 7:00 in the morning.

2. I _____ my teeth and _____ a shower.

3. I _____ dressed.

4. I _____ breakfast.

5. I _____ the newspaper.

6. I _____ to work at 8:30.

7. I _____ the train to my office.

8. I _____ from 9:00 until 6:00.

9. I _____ lunch at 12:30 in the afternoon.

10. I _____ work at 6:00 in the evening.

11. I _____ home at 6:30.

12. I _____ dinner with my family at 7:00.

13. During dinner we _____ about our day.

14. After dinner we _____ the dishes and then _____ television.

15. The kids _____ their homework and _____ to music.

Hello! How Are You?   Big or Small? Short or Tall?   Everyday Life

This Is My Family   Welcome to My Home!

16. My wife and I _____ before bed.

17. We _____ to sleep at 11:30 at night.

ANSWER KEY
1. wake; 2. brush, take; 3. get; 4. eat/have; 5. read; 6. go; 7. take; 8. work; 9. eat/have; 10. leave; 11. get; 12. eat; 13. talk; 14. do, watch; 15. do, listen; 16. read; 17. go

---

Take It Further

▶ 5C Take It Further (CD 2, Track 3)

Let's review the days of the week.

Monday	
Tuesday	
Wednesday	
Thursday	
Friday	
Saturday	
Sunday	

There are seven days in a week.	
The work week has five days.	
Monday is the first day of the work week.	
There are two days in the weekend: Saturday and Sunday.	

Let's look at the verbs start and end, and the time expressions before, during, and after.

The work week starts on Monday.	
The work week ends on Friday.	
Monday is before Tuesday.	
Wednesday is after Tuesday.	

Tuesday and Wednesday are during the work week.	

Grammar Builder 1

▶ 5D Grammar Builder 1 (CD 2, Track 4)

TELLING TIME

What time is it? For the hour, just use the number and o'clock.

It's one o'clock.	1:00
It's seven o'clock.	7:00

For the half-hour, use the number **thirty**, or **half past**.

It's five thirty. It's half past five.	5:30
It's ten thirty. It's half past ten.	10:30

For the quarter hour, use the number **fifteen**, **quarter past**, or **quarter after**. The article, **a**, as in **a quarter past**, is optional but you may hear it said by some people.

It's four fifteen. It's (a) quarter past four. It's (a) quarter after four.	4:15
It's eight fifteen. It's (a) quarter past eight. It's (a) quarter after eight.	8:15

For three quarters past the hour, use **forty-five**, or **quarter to** with the next hour.

It's nine forty-five. It's (a) quarter to ten.	9:45

Hello! How Are You?   Big or Small? Short or Tall?   Everyday Life

This Is My Family   Welcome to My Home!

It's two forty-five. It's (a) quarter to three.	2:45

For other times, just use the number.

It's one twenty.	1:20
It's three twenty-five.	3:25
It's six fifty-five.	6:55

You can also use after/past or to.

It's twenty after two. It's twenty past two.	2:20
It's ten after three. It's ten past three.	3:10
It's twenty to seven.	6:40
It's ten to nine.	8:50

Other time expressions are:

It's noon.	12:00 p.m.
It's midnight.	12:00 a.m.
It's nine in the morning.	9:00 a.m.
It's three in the afternoon.	3:00 p.m.
It's six in the evening.	6:00 p.m.
It's ten at night.	10:00 p.m.

You may also hear someone say a.m. or p.m. instead of morning, afternoon, evening, and night.

It's nine thirty a.m.	9:30 a.m.
It's three p.m.	3:00 p.m.
It's six forty-five p.m.	6:45 p.m.
It's ten p.m.	10:00 p.m.

Use **what time** in questions, and **at** in answers.

What time do you wake up?	
I wake up at seven thirty in the morning.	
What time do you have dinner?	
We have dinner at seven thirty in the evening.	

Vocabulary Builder 2

▶ 5E Vocabulary Builder 2 (CD 2, Track 5)

During the week, John wakes up early for work.	
But on the weekend, he sleeps late.	
He gets up at nine thirty.	
He watches TV while he eats/has breakfast.	
Then he goes to the gym.	
After the gym, John goes running in the park.	
In the afternoon, John reads magazines or uses the computer.	
He reads and writes e-mails to his friends and family.	
On Saturday nights, John sees his friends.	
They go to a restaurant or to the movies.	

Hello! How Are You?   Big or Small? Short or Tall?   Everyday Life

This Is My Family   Welcome to My Home!

John gets home late on Saturday nights.	
He goes to bed after midnight or at one o'clock in the morning.	
On Sunday mornings, John stays in bed until ten o'clock.	
John works hard during the week, but he relaxes on the weekend.	

✎ Vocabulary Practice 2

▶ 5F Vocabulary Practice 2 (CD 2, Track 6)

Listen, again, and write the verbs that you hear.

1. During the week, John _____ up early for work.

2. But on the weekend, he _____ late.

3. He _____ up at nine thirty.

4. He _____ TV while he _____ breakfast.

5. Then he _____ to the gym.

6. After the gym, John _____ running in the park.

7. In the afternoon, John _____ magazines or _____ the computer.

8. He _____ and _____ e-mails to his friends and family.

9. On Saturday nights, John _____ his friends.

10. They _____ to a restaurant or to the movies.

11. John _____ home late on Saturday nights.

12. He _____ to bed after midnight or one o'clock in the morning.

13. On Sunday mornings, John _____ in bed until ten o'clock.

14. John _____ hard during the week, but he _____

on the weekend.

ANSWER KEY

1. wakes; 2. sleeps; 3. gets; 4. watches, eats; 5. goes; 6. goes; 7. reads, uses; 8. reads, writes;
9. sees; 10. go; 11. gets; 12. goes; 13. stays; 14. works, relaxes

Grammar Builder 2

▶ 5G Grammar Builder 2 (CD 2, Track 7)

VERBS IN THE PRESENT TENSE

In the present tense, just add –s or –es for **he, she,** or **it** forms of a verb. Most
verbs add –s.

I work	we work
you work	you work
he, she, it works	they work

I work at the university.	
We see our friends on the weekend.	
Mary reads e-mail on her computer.	
They get home very late on Saturday nights.	

Verbs that end in –ch, –sh, –x, –z, and –s add –es in the **he, she,** and **it** forms.

He watches TV at night.	
She relaxes on the weekend.	
John brushes his teeth before he takes a shower.	

Hello! How Are You?   Big or Small? Short or Tall?   Everyday Life

This Is My Family   Welcome to My Home!

Verbs that end in –o add –es too, but it sounds like z.

The student does her homework.	
Jack goes to the movies with his friends.	

Remember that nouns that end in –y change to –ies in the plural: **city, cities**; **university, universities**. Verbs that end in –y take –ies in the **he, she, it** forms.

John studies English literature at the university.	

✎ Work Out 1

▶ 5H Work Out 1 (CD 2, Track 8)

Listen and write the verb forms that you hear.

1. It _____ Saturday, so John _____ in bed late.

2. On Monday, we _____ up early and _____ to work.

3. Professor Wheaton _____ twenty three students. They _____ English literature.

4. Peter _____ the computer in the evening.

5. He _____ e-mails and _____ the newspaper.

6. Mr. Archer _____ with his family on the weekend.

7. People _____ the train or the bus to work.

8. I _____ home at six o'clock in the evening.

9. Sarah _____ lunch and _____ TV.

10. The children _____ in their bedroom.

11. We _____ to the movies on Friday night and _____ home on Saturday night.

12. Joe _____ up and _____ his teeth.

13. You _____ to music and _____ your homework.

14. The students _____ to their professor.

ANSWER KEY

1. is, stays; 2. get, go; 3. has, study; 4. uses; 5. writes, reads; 6. relaxes; 7. take; 8. get;
9. eats, watches; 10. sleep; 11. go, stay; 12. gets, brushes; 13. listen, do; 14. talk

Bring It All Together

▶ 5I Bring It All Together (CD 2, Track 9)

Now let's bring it all together, and add a little bit more vocabulary and structure. Bob and Susan are at the supermarket. Listen to their conversation.

Bob:	Hey, Susan. How's it going?
Susan:	Hi Bob! Good to see you. What's new? How are Diana and the kids?
Bob:	They're good. Diana has a new job, and the kids are in school.
Susan:	A new job? That's great. But today is Friday. You're not at the office?
Bob:	Oh, no, I don't work on Fridays. I have Fridays off.
Susan:	You have Fridays off? A three-day weekend every week? Lucky you!
Bob:	Yeah, it's great. Diana goes to work, the kids go to school, and I stay home and do nothing!
Susan:	Come on, Bob. That's not true. You're here at the supermarket!
Bob:	You're right. After I bring the kids to school, I come to the supermarket and buy food for the family for the weekend.
Susan:	So, you bring the kids to school, and then go food shopping.
Bob:	Well, after I bring the kids to school, I go to the post office.

Hello! How Are You?   Big or Small? Short or Tall?   **Everyday Life**

This Is My Family   Welcome to My Home!

Susan:	And after you go food shopping, you go home and relax?
Bob:	Um, no, not really. After I go food shopping I go home and clean the house.
Susan:	And then you relax? You read or watch television?
Bob:	No, then I do laundry.
Susan:	And after you do laundry, you relax?
Bob:	No, then I start to cook, and after that, I . . .
Susan:	Bob, you don't have a three-day weekend. You don't have Fridays off.
Bob:	I don't?
Susan:	No, you work a lot on Fridays.
Bob:	Hmm. I think you're right!
Susan:	Well, Bob, enjoy the rest of your "day off"!
Bob:	Gee, thanks a lot, Susan!

Take It Further

▶ 5J Take It Further (CD 2, Track 10)

Remember that **not** (negative) sentences with the verb **have** use **do** or **does**.

I have a big family.	
I do not have a big family. I don't have a big family.	
She has a little brother.	
She does not have a little brother. She doesn't have a little brother.	

Other verbs (**work, relax, stay**) also use **do** or **does** in the negative with **not**.

Bob works on Thursdays. Bob doesn't work on Fridays.	
Joan relaxes on the weekend. Joan doesn't relax during the week.	

| Diana and Bob stay home on Saturdays. They don't stay home on Mondays. | |

Do you see the –s/–es ending of the **he, she, it** form? In the positive (**yes**) sentence, it's on the verb:

Bob works.	
Joan relaxes.	

But in the negative (**not**) sentence, it's on **does**. The verb does not have the –s/–es ending:

Bob does not work.

Joan does not relax.

We'll see more about **do** and **does** in negatives and questions in Lesson 6.

✎ Work Out 2

Let's practice telling time. Answer the question: **What time is it?**

Example: 1:00
Answer: **It's one o'clock.**

1. 9:00 _____

2. 10:15 _____

3. 8:30 _____

4. 7:45 _____

5. 12:00 p.m. _____

Hello! How Are You?   Big or Small? Short or Tall?   Everyday Life

This Is My Family   Welcome to My Home!

6. 12:00 a.m. _____

7. 2:10 _____

8. 4:20 _____

9. 10:40 _____

10. 6:55 _____

ANSWER KEY

1. It's nine o'clock. 2. It's ten fifteen./It's (a) quarter past ten./It's (a) quarter after ten. 3. It's eight thirty./It's half past eight. 4. It's seven forty-five./It's (a) quarter to eight. 5. It's twelve o'clock in the afternoon./It's noon. 6. It's twelve o'clock (at night)./It's midnight. 7. It's two ten./It's ten past two./It's ten after two. 8. It's four twenty./It's twenty after four./It's twenty past four. 9. It's ten forty./It's twenty to eleven. 10. It's six fifty-five./It's five to seven.

Great. Now choose the correct verb form.

1. Brad (**wake/wakes**) up very early in the morning.

2. They (**eat/eats**) at a Thai restaurant on Saturdays.

3. I (**work/works**) from Monday to Friday.

4. Their professor doesn't (**work/works**) on Sundays.

5. Miriam (**leave/leaves**) the office at 5:30.

6. The boy (**get/gets**) dressed and then (**eat/eats**) breakfast.

7. We (**have/has**) dinner before we (**watch/watches**) television.

8. You (**take/takes**) the train to work.

9. My sister doesn't (**listen/listens**) to music while she (**do/does**) homework.

10. Bob (**relax/relaxes**) during the weekend, but doesn't (**relax/relaxes**) during the week.

ANSWER KEY

1. **wakes**; 2. **eat**; 3. **work**; 4. **work**; 5. **leaves**; 6. **gets, eats**; 7. **have, watch**; 8. **take**; 9. **listen, does**;
10. **relaxes, relax**

✎ Drive It Home

Let's practice verbs. Rewrite the sentences with the new subjects.

1. We wake up early on Mondays. (He …)

   _____

2. I eat breakfast at nine thirty in the morning. (Susan …)

   _____

3. You take the bus to work. (Bill …)

   _____

4. They have lunch at twelve thirty in the afternoon. (Mrs. Ramirez …)

   _____

5. I work at the university. (The professor …)

   _____

6. We watch television after we eat dinner. (She …)

   _____

7. The boys brush their teeth before bed. (The boy …)

   _____

8. They go to bed early during the week. (John …)

   _____

Hello! How Are You?   Big or Small? Short or Tall?   Everyday Life

This Is My Family   Welcome to My Home!

ANSWER KEY

1. He wakes up early on Monday. 2. Susan eats breakfast at nine thirty in the morning. 3. Bill takes the bus to work. 4. Mrs. Ramirez has lunch at twelve thirty in the afternoon. 5. The professor works at the university. 6. She watches television after she eats dinner. 7. The boy brushes his teeth before bed. 8. John goes to bed early during the week.

Parting Words

Congratulations! You finished another lesson of Essential English. Do you know:

☐ the days of the week? (No? Go back to 110.)

☐ how to tell time? (No? Go back to 111.)

☐ common verbs for everyday life? (No? Go back to 113.)

☐ how to use verbs in the present tense? (No? Go back to 115.)

☐ how to put it all together in a short conversation about a typical day?
(No? Go back to 117.)

Don't forget to practice and reinforce what you've learned by visiting www.livinglanguage.com/languagelab for flashcards, games, and quizzes!

Word Recall

Choose the right verb.

1. I (**wake/take/have**) up very early during the week.

2. She (**washes/does/brushes**) her teeth.

3. You (**do/take/make**) a shower in the morning.

4. Bill (**does/gets/takes**) dressed after his shower.

5. They (**read/write/eat**) the newspaper every morning.

6. Professor Wheaton (**goes/takes/does**) to work at ten in the morning.

7. You (**go/take/watch**) the train to your office.

8. Bob (**works/relaxes/sleeps**) in his office from nine o'clock until six o'clock.

9. They (**go/leave/take**) work at six o'clock in the evening.

10. Mary (**works/does/gets**) home at seven in the evening.

11. We (**have/do/read**) dinner with friends at a restaurant.

12. He (**makes/talks/writes**) with his wife about his day.

13. The kids (**watch/listen/read**) television after their homework.

14. We (**have/do/take**) the dishes in the sink.

15. They (**have/do/go**) to sleep early during the week.

ANSWER KEY
1. wake; 2. brushes; 3. take; 4. gets; 5. read; 6. goes; 7. take; 8. works; 9. leave; 10. gets; 11. have; 12. talks; 13. watch; 14. do; 15. go

QUIZ 1

Now let's see how you've done so far. In this section you'll find a short quiz testing what you learned in Lessons 1-5. After you've answered all of the questions, score your quiz and see how you did! If you find that you need to go back and review, please do so before continuing on to Lesson 6.

You'll get a second quiz after Lesson 10, followed by a final review with five dialogues and comprehension questions.

Let's get started!

A. Which room?

1. The sink is in . . .   a. the bedroom.
2. The bed is in . . .   b. the dining room.
3. The couch is in . . .   c. the bathroom.
4. The table and chairs are in . . .   d. the kitchen.
5. The shower is in . . .   e. the living room.

B. Give the plurals.

1. one boy, two _____

2. one room, three _____

3. one woman, four _____

4. one city, five _____

5. one child, three _____

C. Fill in the blanks with am, is, are, have, or has.

1. They _____ a small house.

2. _____ you the new professor?

3. Mary _____ in her bedroom.

4. Richard _____ three children.

5. I _____ American.

D. Choose the right verb form.

1. We (watch/watches) television every night.

2. Greg (relax/relaxes) during the weekend.

3. You (take/takes) the train to work.

4. She doesn't (works/work) in an office.

5. They (doesn't/don't) have dinner before six thirty.

E. Complete the sentences with the, a, or an.

1. There is _____ new professor at the university.

2. I have a dog. _____ dog's name is Max.

3. _____ Eiffel Tower is in Paris.

4. Marjorie is _____ excellent student.

5. Do you have _____ question?

ANSWER KEY
A. 1. d; 2. a; 3. e; 4. b; 5. c
B. 1. boys; 2. rooms; 3. women; 4. cities; 5. children
C. 1. have; 2. Are; 3. is; 4. has; 5. am
D. 1. watch; 2. relaxes; 3. take; 4. work; 5. don't
E. 1. a; 2. The; 3. The; 4. an; 5. a

How Did You Do?

Give yourself a point for every correct answer, then use the following key to determine whether or not you're ready to move on:

0-10 points: It's probably best to go back and study the lessons again to make sure you understood everything completely. Take your time; it's not a race! Make sure you spend time reviewing the vocabulary and reading through each Grammar Builder section carefully.

11-18 points: If the questions you missed were in section A, you may want to review the vocabulary from previous lessons again; if you missed answers mostly in sections B, C, D, or E, check the Grammar Builder sections to make sure you have your grammar basics down.

19-25 points: Feel free to move on to Lesson 6! You're doing a great job.

☐☐ **points**

Lesson 6:
Around Town

Welcome back! This lesson is about places in a town or city. So, you'll learn:

☐ basic vocabulary for places in a **town** or **city**

☐ how to use **do** and **does** in questions and with **not**

☐ more vocabulary for around town

☐ how to use question words

☐ how to put it all together and ask for directions

Let's start with some new vocabulary and expressions.

Hello! How Are You?   Big or Small? Short or Tall?   Everyday Life

This Is My Family   Welcome to My Home!

Vocabulary Builder 1

▶ 6A Vocabulary Builder 1 (CD 2, Track 11)

Where is the bank?	
The bank is on Main Street.	
There is an ATM in front of the bank.	
People get money at the ATM.	
Across the street from the bank is the post office.	
People buy stamps and mail letters at the post office.	
Next to the post office is a small grocery store.	
People buy food at the grocery store.	
Down the street there is a clothing store.	
People buy clothes there.	
There's a restaurant near the clothing store.	
And there's a gas station with a convenience store on Main Street.	
People get gas for their cars at the gas station.	
They buy coffee, newspapers, and magazines at the convenience store.	

✎ Vocabulary Practice 1

Let's practice the vocabulary you've learned. **Where do you …**

1. … buy stamps and mail letters?   a. At a bank.

2. … get money?   b. At a clothing store.

3. … get gas and newspapers?   c. At a post office.

4. … buy food?   d. At a restaurant.

5. … eat dinner?   e. At a convenience store.

6. … buy clothes?   f. At a grocery store.

ANSWER KEY
1. c; 2. a; 3. e; 4. f; 5.d; 6. b

Let's practice some verbs that you use when you talk about your town.

1. People _____ money at a bank or an ATM.

2. People _____ letters at the post office.

3. People _____ food at a grocery store and clothes at a clothing store.

4. People _____ gas for their cars at the gas station.

ANSWER KEY
1. get; 2. mail; 3. buy; 4. get/buy

Take It Further

▶ 6B Take It Further 1 (CD 2, Track 12)

GET

The verb get is used in a lot of expressions you've learned so far. Let's review them, and add a few more.

Hello! How Are You?   Big or Small? Short or Tall?   Everyday Life

This Is My Family   Welcome to My Home!

I get dressed after I shower.	
I get undressed before I go to bed.	

Get (to) is also used with places, meaning arrive at or go to.

Bill gets to the office at nine o'clock in the morning.	
The students get to class at one o'clock in the afternoon.	
How do you get to work? By car or by train?	
Mary gets home at six in the evening.	

Get also means to buy or to obtain.

People get money at the ATM.	
John gets gas at the gas station.	
You get newspapers and magazines at the convenience store.	

Get also means become.

The children get sleepy at nine o'clock, and then they go to bed.	
In Boston, the days get cold in December.	
The days get hot in August.	

Get is a very common verb in English. We'll see more in later lessons.

Grammar Builder 1

▶ 6C Grammar Builder 1 (CD 2, Track 13)

DO AND DOES

Remember to use do (with I, you, we, and they) or does (with he, she, or it) in the negative (not) form of all verbs except be. Do + not is shortened to don't, and does + not is shortened to doesn't.

You work at a bank. You do not work at a bank. You don't work at a bank.	
We eat dinner at the restaurant. We do not eat dinner at the restaurant. We don't eat dinner at the restaurant.	

The he, she, and it forms of verbs take –s or –es: takes, goes, fixes. But in the negative, the –s or –es is on does, and so the verb doesn't have an ending: doesn't take, doesn't go, doesn't fix.

She buys food at the grocery store. She does not buy food at the grocery store. She doesn't buy food at the grocery store.	
He gets stamps at the post office. He does not get stamps at the post office. He doesn't get stamps at the post office.	

Hello! How Are You?   Big or Small? Short or Tall?   Everyday Life

This Is My Family   Welcome to My Home!

Remember that the negative of **be** only uses **not**. In negative **be** sentences, **be** is contracted with the pronoun (**you + are = you're**; **she + is = she's**), or **not** is contracted with **be** (**are + not = aren't**; **is + not = isn't**).

You're at the post office. You're not at the post office. You aren't at the post office.	
She's at the grocery store. She's not at the grocery store. She isn't at the grocery store.	

Don't forget that with the pronoun **I**, you can contract the negative only one way.

I'm at the office. I'm not at the office.	

To form a question with **be**, just change the order of the subject and the verb.

New York is a big city. Is New York a big city?	
Bill is at his office. Is Bill at his office?	

But all verbs except **be** use **do** or **does** in questions.

They have dinner at seven o'clock. Do they have dinner at seven o'clock?	
You work at a bank. Do you work at a bank?	
She lives in a small town. Does she live in a small town?	
He goes to work by train. Does he go to work by train?	

There are many common expressions with do.

The children do their homework after dinner.	
We do the dishes after we eat.	
Sarah is a good student; she does well at school.	
Max isn't a good student; he doesn't do well at school.	

Vocabulary Builder 2

▶ 6D Vocabulary Builder 2 (CD 2, Track 14)

New York is a very big city.	
There are many tall buildings in New York.	
The Empire State Building is a famous building.	
It is at the intersection of Fifth Avenue and Thirty-Fourth Street.	
There are very many streets with a lot of taxis, cars, and buses.	
People in New York live in apartments.	
They buy food in supermarkets or food stores.	
People shop for clothes and other things at department stores.	
Macy's and Bloomingdale's are famous department stores.	

Hello! How Are You?   Big or Small? Short or Tall?   Everyday Life

This Is My Family   Welcome to My Home!

People get bread at bakeries.	
They get meat at butcher shops.	
There are many schools and universities in New York, too.	
Many people work in office buildings.	
They get to work by subway, by bus, by taxi, or on foot.	
There are big libraries with many books and computers.	
There are many churches, synagogues, and mosques in New York.	
On weekends, many New Yorkers go to parks and relax.	
They also go to restaurants or to the movies.	

✎ Vocabulary Practice 2

Now let's practice the new vocabulary. Fill in the blanks. Listen to your audio again if you need help.

1. New York is a very big _____ .

2. There are many tall _____ in New York.

3. The Empire State Building is a _____ building.

4. It is at the _____ of Fifth Avenue and Thirty-Fourth

   Street.

5. There are very many _____ with a lot of taxis, cars, and buses.

6. People in New York live in _____.

7. They buy food in _____ or food stores.

8. People shop for clothes and other things at _____ stores.

9. Macy's and Bloomingdale's are _____ department stores.

10. People get bread at _____.

11. They get meat at _____ shops.

12. There are many _____ and universities in New York, too.

13. Many people work in _____ buildings.

14. They _____ to work by subway, by bus, by taxi, or on foot.

15. There are big _____ with many books and computers.

16. There are many _____, synagogues, and mosques in New York.

17. On weekends, many New Yorkers go to _____ and relax.

18. They also go to restaurants or to the _____.

ANSWER KEY
1. city; 2. buildings; 3. famous; 4. intersection; 5. streets; 6. apartments; 7. supermarkets;
8. department; 9. famous; 10. bakeries; 11. butcher; 12. schools; 13. office; 14. get; 15. libraries;
16. churches; 17. parks; 18. movies

Hello! How Are You?   Big or Small? Short or Tall?   Everyday Life

This Is My Family   Welcome to My Home!

Grammar Builder 2

▶ 6E Grammar Builder 2 (CD 2, Track 15)

QUESTIONS AND QUESTION WORDS

You already know how to ask yes/no questions with be.

The children are at the park. Are the children at the park?	
Mrs. Ramirez is a great professor. Is Mrs. Ramirez a great professor?	

With have and all other verbs, use do or does in yes/no questions. Don't forget that the he/she/it form of the verb does not take –(e)s with does.

They have a big family. Do they have a big family?	
John has a new computer. Does John have a new computer?	
Susan works in the city. Does Susan work in the city?	

You can also ask questions with question words.

What?	
What does John do in the morning? He eats breakfast in the morning.	
Who?	
Who do the students see in class? They see their professor in class.	
When?	

When does the train leave? The train leaves at 9:05 in the morning.	
Where?	
Where do Bill and Cynthia live? They live in Chicago.	
How?	
How do you get to work? I get to work by bus.	
Why?	
Why do you buy bread at the bakery? I buy bread at the bakery because it is good.	

✎ Work Out 1

▶ 6F Work Out 1 (CD 2, Track 16)

Listen and write the words you hear.

1. _____ does Maria work?

2. She _____ at the university.

3. _____ does she do?

4. She _____ Spanish.

5. _____ does she have class?

6. She _____ class at one o'clock in the afternoon.

7. _____ does she teach?

8. She teaches _____.

Hello! How Are You?   Big or Small? Short or Tall?   Everyday Life

This Is My Family   Welcome to My Home!

9. _____ does she get to work?

10. She gets to work _____.

ANSWER KEY
1. **Where;** 2. **works;** 3. **What;** 4. **teaches;** 5. **When;** 6 **has;** 7. **Who;** 8. **students;** 9. **How;** 10. **by car**

Bring It All Together

▶ 6G Bring It All Together (CD 2, Track 17)

Mira and Hector are students in a Spanish class. Listen in as Mira asks Hector about his town.

Mira:	Do you live in a big city or a small town, Hector?
Hector:	I live in a town. It's not small, but it's not very big.
Mira:	Is it far from the university?
Hector:	Yes, it's in New York.
Mira:	But New York is a big city!
Hector:	New York is also a state. I live in a town in New York state.
Mira:	Oh, right. Is your town near New York City?
Hector:	It's about two hours away from the city. There are trains and buses that go to the city. My father works in the city. He takes the train to the city very early every morning.
Mira:	Who do you live with?
Hector:	I live with my mother and father, and I have two sisters.
Mira:	Are there a lot of stores in your town?
Hector:	Yes, there's a supermarket, clothing stores, a bakery, a butcher shop, a department store, and three or four convenience stores.
Mira:	Do you live in the center of town?
Hector:	No, there aren't many houses in the center of town. There are a lot of stores, restaurants, a few banks, a park, the school, the post office, some churches, and a few apartment buildings, but not many houses.
Mira:	Do you go home often?

Hector:	I go home and see my family once or twice each semester.
Mira:	How do you get home?
Hector:	I go home by train usually.
Mira:	And what do you do?
Hector:	I relax, I spend time with my family, and I see my friends.
Mira:	That's nice. I come from Croatia, so I don't go home very often.
Hector:	And where in Croatia do you come from?
Mira:	I come from Zagreb.
Hector:	Is that a small town?
Mira:	No, it's a city. It's the capital of the country.
Hector:	And why are you studying Spanish?
Mira:	I'm studying Spanish because I like the language a lot, and because many people speak Spanish. It's a useful language. And why are you studying Spanish? Isn't Hector a Spanish name?
Hector:	Yes, Hector is a Spanish name. My family is originally from Mexico.
Mira:	You don't speak Spanish already?
Hector:	No, I don't. My sisters and I only speak English. My parents speak English and Spanish, and my grandparents only speak Spanish.
Mira:	So you're studying Spanish because your family is from Mexico?
Hector:	Yes, that's right. And also because it's a useful second language in the United States.

Take It Further

▶ 6H Take It Further (CD 2, Track 18)

Did you notice in the conversation that Hector asks Mira:

Why are you studying Spanish?	

You already know the simple present tense:

I study Spanish at the university.	

Hello! How Are You?   Big or Small? Short or Tall?   Everyday Life

This Is My Family   Welcome to My Home!

We eat dinner at seven in the evening.	

Use the simple present tense to talk about actions that happen in general. Use the simple present tense with phrases like generally, usually, always, on Monday, every day, at seven o'clock, and so on.

Hector's grandparents always speak Spanish.	
Hector's mother speaks English with her children, but she speaks Spanish with her parents.	
Hector studies Spanish every Monday, Wednesday, and Friday.	
Hector usually sees his family once or twice each semester.	

Use the be + ing present (called the present progressive or present continuous) to talk about actions that are happening now.

You are studying English right now.	
You are reading a sentence in English.	
Mira is in Croatia now, so she's speaking Croatian. (But she also speaks English.)	
Hector's mother is with her children now, so she's speaking English. (But she also speaks Spanish.)	

We'll come back to the present progressive later.

✎ Work Out 2

Give the negative (not) of each sentence.

Example: I work in a bank.
Answer: **I do not/don't work in a bank.**

1. She goes to work by train.

   _____

2. The professor teaches every Wednesday.

   _____

3. We eat at the restaurant every Friday.

   _____

4. I get gas at the gas station in the morning.

   _____

5. John buys bread at the bakery.

   _____

6. She buys milk at the convenience store.

   _____

7. They get stamps at the post office.

   _____

8. Bill is at the bank.

   _____

ANSWER KEY
1. **She does not go/doesn't go to work by train. 2. The professor does not teach/doesn't teach every Wednesday. 3. We do not eat/don't eat at the restaurant every Friday. 4. I do not get/don't get gas**

Hello! How Are You?   Big or Small? Short or Tall?   Everyday Life

This Is My Family   Welcome to My Home!

at the gas station in the morning. **5.** John does not buy/doesn't buy bread at the bakery. **6.** She does not buy/doesn't buy milk at the convenience store. **7.** They do not get/don't get stamps at the post office. **8.** Bill is not/isn't at the bank.

Great. Now form questions.

Example: Bill works <u>at a clothing store.</u>
Answer: **Where does Bill work?**

1. Mira studies <u>Spanish</u> at the university.

   _____

2. Hector sees <u>his friends</u> at home.

   _____

3. The train leaves <u>at 9:05 a.m.</u>

   _____

4. Hector's father goes to work in the city <u>by train.</u>

   _____

5. Jasmine lives <u>in a small town.</u>

   _____

6. They buy milk at the convenience store because it's <u>near their apartment.</u>

   _____

ANSWER KEY
1. What does Mira study at the university? **2.** Who does Hector see at home? **3.** When does the train leave? (Or: What time does the train leave?) **4.** How does Hector's father go to work in the city? **5.** Where does Jasmine live? **6.** Why do they buy milk at the convenience store?

✎ Drive It Home

For each sentence, give the negative (**not**), the **yes/no** question, and the question with a question word.

Example: Hank works at a gas station.
Answer: **Hank doesn't work at a gas station.**
Does Hank work at a gas station?
Where does Hank work?

1. Bob and Mary live in a big house.

2. They buy their food at the supermarket.

3. The students see their professor every morning.

4. Gloria leaves work at 5:45.

5. Joe goes to work by bus.

6. You eat at the restaurant because the food is good.

ANSWER KEY

1. Bob and Mary don't live in a big house. Do Bob and Mary live in a big house? Where do Bob and Mary live? **2.** They don't buy their food at the supermarket. Do they buy their food at the supermarket? What do they buy at the supermarket? **3.** The students don't see their professor every morning. Do the students see their professor every morning? Who do the students see every morning? **4.** Gloria doesn't leave work at 5:45. Does Gloria leave work at 5:45? When (What time) does Gloria leave work? **5.** Joe doesn't go to work by bus. Does Joe go to work by bus? How does Joe go to work? **6.** You don't eat at the restaurant because the food is good. Do you eat at the restaurant because the food is good? Why do you eat at the restaurant?

Hello! How Are You?   Big or Small? Short or Tall?   Everyday Life

This Is My Family   Welcome to My Home!

Parting Words

Well done! You just finished Lesson Six. How did you do? Do you know:

- ☐ basic vocabulary for places in a **town** or **city**? (No? Go back to 128.)
- ☐ how to use **do** and **does** in questions and with **not**? (No? Go back to 131.)
- ☐ more vocabulary for around town? (No? Go back to 133.)
- ☐ how to use question words? (No? Go back to 136.)
- ☐ how to put it all together in a dialogue? (No? Go back to 138.)

Don't forget to practice and reinforce what you've learned by visiting www.livinglanguage.com/languagelab for flashcards, games, and quizzes!

Word Recall

Fill in each blank with the best answer.

1. People get money at the _____.

2. People buy _____ and mail _____ at the post office.

3. People buy food at the _____ store or

   _____.

4. People buy clothes at the _____ store.

5. People eat at the _____.

6. People get gas at the _____.

7. People buy coffee, newspapers, and magazines at the

   _____ store.

8. There are tall _____ in cities.

9. The Empire State Building is at the _____ of Fifth

   Avenue and Thirty-Fourth Street.

10. There are cars, taxis, and buses on the _____.

11. People in cities often live in _____, not houses.

12. People shop for clothes and other things at _____ stores.

13. People get bread at the _____.

14. People get meat at the _____ shop.

Hello! How Are You?   Big or Small? Short or Tall?   Everyday Life

This Is My Family   Welcome to My Home!

15. In cities, many people work in _____ buildings.

16. People in cities get to work by _____, by bus, by taxi, or on foot.

17. There are many books and computers in _____.

18. In cities, many people go to _____ to walk or relax.

ANSWER KEY

1. bank or ATM; 2. stamps, letters; 3. grocery or food, supermarket; 4. clothing; 5. restaurant;
6. gas station; 7. convenience; 8. buildings; 9. intersection; 10. street/streets; 11. apartments;
12. department; 13. bakery; 14. butcher; 15. office; 16. subway/train; 17. libraries; 18. parks

Lesson 7:
Let's Eat!

In this lesson, we'll go to a restaurant. That means you'll learn:

☐ basic vocabulary for meals and restaurants

☐ how to make polite requests

☐ basic food vocabulary

☐ how to use **some** and **any**

☐ how to put it all together when ordering food at a restaurant

Let's get started. **Enjoy the meal!**

Hello! How Are You?   Big or Small? Short or Tall?   Everyday Life

This Is My Family   Welcome to My Home!

Vocabulary Builder 1

▶ 7A Vocabulary Builder 1 (CD 2, Track 19)

People eat breakfast in the morning.	
People often eat eggs, toast, or cereal for breakfast.	
People eat lunch around noon.	
People often eat sandwiches for lunch.	
People eat dinner in the evening.	
Dinner is usually a big meal.	
People eat with a fork, knife, and spoon.	
The food is on a plate, and the drink is in a glass.	
Before the meal at a restaurant, the server gives customers the menu.	
People first choose an appetizer.	
Appetizers are usually salads or small dishes.	
After the appetizer, the server brings the main course.	
The main course is usually meat, pasta, or vegetables.	
After the main course, some people eat dessert.	
Dessert is usually cake, pie, or ice cream.	

People often drink coffee or tea with dessert.	
After the meal, the server brings the bill.	

Take it Further

▶ 7B Take It Further (CD 2, Track 20)

You **eat** or **have** a meal.

People eat breakfast in the morning. People have breakfast in the morning.	
People eat lunch around noon. People have lunch around noon.	
People eat dinner in the evening. People have dinner in the evening.	

Another word for **dinner** is **supper**.

What time do you usually have supper?	

Another word for **appetizer** is **starter**.

Are you having a starter before the main course?	

Another word for **bill** is **check**.

At the end of a meal, the customer says "check, please!" or "could we please have the bill?"	

Hello! How Are You?   Big or Small? Short or Tall?   Everyday Life

This Is My Family   Welcome to My Home!

A **server** is either a man or a woman. A server who is a man is also called a **waiter**, and a server who is a woman is called a **waitress**.

The waiter brings us the menu.	
We ask the waitress for the check.	

✎ Vocabulary Practice 1

Fill in the blanks with the correct vocabulary word.

1. People eat _____ in the morning.

2. People often eat eggs, toast, or _____ for breakfast.

3. People eat _____ around noon.

4. People often eat _____ for lunch.

5. People eat _____ in the evening.

6. Dinner is usually a big _____.

7. People eat with a _____, _____ and spoon, and drink from a

   _____.

8. Before the meal at a restaurant, the server gives customers the _____.

9. People first choose an _____.

10. Appetizers are usually salads or small _____.

11. After the appetizer, the server brings the _____ course.

12. The main course is usually _____, pasta, or vegetables.

13. After the main course, some people eat _____.

14. Dessert is usually _____, pie, or ice cream.

15. People often drink coffee or _____ with dessert.

16. After the meal, the server brings the _____.

ANSWER KEY
1. breakfast; 2. cereal; 3. lunch; 4. sandwiches; 5. dinner/supper; 6. meal; 7. fork, knife, glass;
8. menu; 9. appetizer; 10. dishes; 11. main; 12. meat; 13. dessert; 14. cake; 15. tea; 16. bill/check

⊕ Culture Note

Many Americans love to eat out (eat in a restaurant). In America, people like to eat many different cuisines (cooking traditions), such as French, Italian, Chinese, Spanish, Mexican, Japanese, and Korean cuisine, and many more. When people eat out in America, they leave the server a tip (a payment for good service). If the service is excellent, the tip is usually 20% of the total bill. If the service is good, the tip is 15%. Also, when American friends eat in restaurants, they usually split (divide) the bill. This is sometimes called going Dutch.

Grammar Builder 1

▶ 7C Grammar Builder 1 (CD 2, Track 21)

POLITE REQUESTS

You can make requests by simply using a verb without the –(e)s ending.
Add please to be more polite.

Please bring the menu.	
Please bring more bread.	
Pass the milk, please.	

Hello! How Are You?   Big or Small? Short or Tall?   Everyday Life

This Is My Family   Welcome to My Home!

To make a request very polite, use the expression could you please ... ?

Could you please bring the menu?	
Could you please pass the salt?	
Could you please bring the check?	

Another polite expression is would like.

I would like the menu, please.	
We would like a table for two.	
Would you like dessert?	

Vocabulary Builder 2

▶ 7D Vocabulary Builder 2 (CD 2, Track 22)

Beef, pork, and lamb are kinds of meat.	
Chicken, duck, and turkey are kinds of poultry.	
Carrots, lettuce, cucumbers, and spinach are vegetables.	
Oranges, apples, bananas, and pears are kinds of fruit.	
People often eat bread with butter on it.	
Italy is famous for pasta dishes, for example, spaghetti with tomato sauce.	

France is famous for cheese and wine.	
Germany is famous for beer.	
People in Japan, China, and Korea eat a lot of rice.	
There is rice and raw fish in sushi.	
Hamburgers, hot dogs, and fries are American fast food.	
Many people drink orange juice, coffee, or tea at breakfast.	

✎ Vocabulary Practice 2

Now let's practice the new vocabulary.

1. What are three examples of meat? _____

2. What are three kinds of poultry? _____

3. Give four examples of vegetables. _____

4. What are four kinds of fruit? _____

5. What do people often put on their bread? _____

6. Spaghetti often comes with what kind of sauce? _____

7. What two things is France famous for? _____

8. What kind of drink is Germany famous for? _____

9. What kind of food do people in Japan, China, and Korea often eat? _____

10. What is there in sushi? _____

Hello! How Are You?   Big or Small? Short or Tall?   Everyday Life

This Is My Family   Welcome to My Home!

11. What are three common American fast foods?_____

12. What are three common breakfast drinks? _____

ANSWER KEY
1. beef, pork, and lamb; 2. chicken, duck, and turkey; 3. carrots, lettuce, cucumbers, and spinach;
4. oranges, apples, bananas, and pears; 5. butter; 6. tomato; 7. wine and cheese; 8. beer; 9. rice;
10. rice and raw fish; 11. hamburgers, hot dogs, and fries; 12. orange juice, coffee, and tea.

Grammar Builder 2

▶ 7E Grammar Builder 2 (CD 2, Track 23)

SOME AND ANY

Use some to talk about amounts that aren't specific or exact.

Please bring me some water.	
We would like some bread.	
I would like some milk and sugar in my coffee.	

If you use some with things that you can count (one person, two people; one student, two students), use some with the plural.

Some people drink red wine, and some people drink white wine.	
There are some tables near the window.	
Some students in the class are excellent, but some are not very good.	

Some is also used in questions to mean an indefinite amount.

Would you like some vegetables?	
Do you have some money for me?	

Any is used in negative (**not**) sentences.

I have <u>some</u> bread. I don't have <u>any</u> bread.	
There are <u>some</u> excellent restaurants in this town. There aren't <u>any</u> excellent restaurants in this town.	
I have <u>some</u> friends from Germany. I don't have <u>any</u> friends from Germany.	

Any is also used in questions.

Would you like any vegetables?	
Do you have any brothers or sisters?	
Does she have any good books?	

✎ Work Out 1

▶ 7F Work Out 1 (CD 2, Track 24)

Listen and write the words you hear.

1. We _____ like a table for two.

2. Are there _____ tables next to the window?

3. _____ you please bring the menu?

4. We don't have _____ forks on the table.

5. We would like _____ bread, please.

6. Pass the salt, _____ .

Hello! How Are You?   Big or Small? Short or Tall?   Everyday Life

This Is My Family   Welcome to My Home!

7. Please bring _____ water.

8. Would you like _____ butter?

9. We would like _____ dessert.

10. Could you please _____ the bill?

ANSWER KEY
1. would; 2. any; 3. Could; 4. any; 5. some; 6. please; 7. some; 8. any; 9. some; 10. bring

🎧 Bring It All Together
▶ 7G Bring It All Together (CD 2, Track 25)

John and Paula are at *Cucina*, a new Italian restaurant in their town. Listen as they order.

Waiter:	Good evening, and welcome to Cucina. Would you like the wine list?
Paula:	Hmmm … No, I don't want any wine, thank you. But I would like some water, please.
John:	Water is good for me, too.
Waiter:	Certainly. Would you like an appetizer?
Paula:	What do you think, John, the bruschetta?
John:	Yes, that sounds good. And maybe the fresh mozzarella plate.
Waiter:	Okay, I'll be right back with some water and your appetizers.
Paula:	So, what are you having?
John:	The roast chicken looks good. But the shrimp looks good, too. I'm not sure.
Paula:	I'd like pasta tonight. The lasagna looks good, but we're having mozzarella as an appetizer.
John:	Yeah, maybe that's too much cheese. How about the spaghetti with the tomato and basil sauce?
Paula:	Yes, that sounds good. Oh, here's our waiter.
Waiter:	So, here are your starters, and two glasses of water. What would you like as a main course, Ma'am?

| Let's Eat! | At Work | Review Dialogues |

Around Town · Let's Go Shopping · What Do You Feel Like Doing?

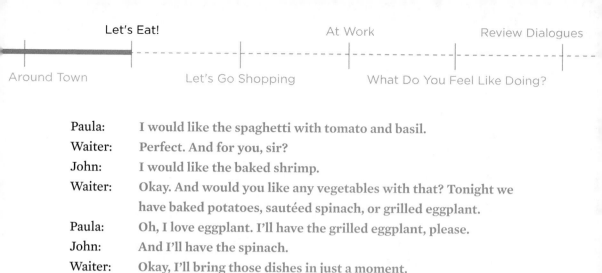

Paula:	I would like the spaghetti with tomato and basil.
Waiter:	Perfect. And for you, sir?
John:	I would like the baked shrimp.
Waiter:	Okay. And would you like any vegetables with that? Tonight we have baked potatoes, sautéed spinach, or grilled eggplant.
Paula:	Oh, I love eggplant. I'll have the grilled eggplant, please.
John:	And I'll have the spinach.
Waiter:	Okay, I'll bring those dishes in just a moment. Enjoy your appetizers!

Take It Further

7H Take it Further (CD 2, Track 26)

Notice the expressions sounds good and looks good. If you hear something and you like it, you say it sounds good.

The music sounds good!	
Mary sounds good when she sings.	
How about some coffee? Oh, yeah. That sounds good.	

If you see something and you like it, you say it looks good.

The cake looks good! I want some.	
There's a new restaurant, and the menu looks really good.	
Your photos of Paris look really good.	

Also notice the phrase too much.

I want one glass of wine. That's two glasses of wine. That's too much wine!	

Hello! How Are You?   Big or Small? Short or Tall?   Everyday Life

This Is My Family   Welcome to My Home!

| Cheese for an appetizer and in the main course? That's too much cheese! | |

We'll come back to **too much, too many, little, a few,** and so on, in the next lesson.

✎ Work Out 2

Let's practice polite requests. Make the following requests more polite, following the example.

Example: Pass the milk, please.
Answer: **Could you please pass the milk?**

1. Bring the menu, please.

   _____

2. Bring some bread, please.

   _____

3. Pass the salt, please.

   _____

4. Read the wine list, please.

   _____

5. Bring a fork and a knife, please.

   _____

ANSWER KEY
1. Could you please bring the menu? 2. Could you please bring some bread? 3. Could you please pass the salt? 4. Could you please read the wine list? 5. Could you please bring a fork and a knife?

Excellent. Now fill in the blanks with some or any.

1. I would like _____ sugar in my tea.

2. We would like _____ bread and butter.

3. We don't have _____ tables near the window.

4. There are _____ very good restaurants in this town.

5. Would you like _____ vegetables with your main courses?

6. Do you have _____ brothers or sisters?

7. I have _____ friends at the university.

8. There aren't _____ Thai restaurants near here.

9. I would like _____ coffee, please.

10. I don't want _____ dessert.

ANSWER KEY
1. some; 2. some; 3. any; 4. some; 5. any; 6. any; 7. some; 8. any; 9. some; 10. any

✎ Drive It Home

Make positive statements with some, negative statements with any, and questions with any, following the example.

Example: There is … cheese in the pasta.
Answers: **There is some cheese in the pasta. There isn't any cheese in the pasta. Is there any cheese in the pasta?**

Hello! How Are You?   Big or Small? Short or Tall?   Everyday Life

This Is My Family   Welcome to My Home!

1. She reads ... books in French.

   _____

2. There is ... sugar in your tea.

   _____

3. They have ... tables next to the windows.

   _____

4. There is ... meat in the dish.

   _____

5. John has ... friends from Canada.

   _____

6. She sees ... people in the library.

   _____

ANSWER KEY

1. She reads some books in French. She doesn't read any books in French. Does she read any books in French? 2. There is some sugar in your tea. There isn't any sugar in your tea. Is there any sugar in your tea? 3. They have some tables next to the windows. They don't have any tables next to the windows. Do they have any tables next to the windows? 4. There is some meat in the dish. There isn't any meat in the dish. Is there any meat in the dish? 5. John has some friends from Canada. John doesn't have any friends from Canada. Does John have any friends from Canada? 6. She sees some people in the library. She doesn't see any people in the library. Does she see any people in the library?

Parting Words

Fantastic! You just finished your seventh lesson of English. Do you know:

- ☐ basic vocabulary for meals and restaurants? (No? Go back to 148.)
- ☐ how to make polite requests? (No? Go back to 151.)
- ☐ basic food vocabulary? (No? Go back to 152.)
- ☐ how to use **some** and **any**? (No? Go back to 154.)
- ☐ how to put it all together when ordering food at a restaurant? (No? Go back to 156.)

Don't forget to practice and reinforce what you've learned by visiting www.livinglanguage.com/languagelab for flashcards, games, and quizzes!

Hello! How Are You?   Big or Small? Short or Tall?   Everyday Life

This Is My Family   Welcome to My Home!

Word Recall

Do you remember the new vocabulary from Lesson 7?

1. People eat _____ in the morning.

2. For breakfast, people often eat _____, toast, or cereal.

3. People eat _____ around noon.

4. For lunch, people often eat _____.

5. People eat _____ in the evening.

6. People use a _____, a _____ and a _____ to eat.

7. People drink from a _____.

8. At a restaurant, people first choose an _____.

9. Then, people choose the _____ course.

10. After the meal, people sometimes eat _____.

11. Beef, _____, and lamb are kinds of meat.

12. _____, duck, and turkey are kinds of poultry.

13. Carrots, lettuce, cucumbers, and spinach are _____.

14. Oranges, apples, bananas, and pears are kinds of _____.

15. People often eat bread with _____ on it.

ANSWER KEY
1. breakfast; 2. eggs; 3. lunch; 4. sandwiches; 5. dinner (or supper); 6. fork, knife, spoon; 7. glass (or cup); 8. appetizer; 9. main; 10. dessert; 11. pork; 12. Chicken; 13. vegetables; 14. fruit; 15. butter

Lesson 8:
Let's Go Shopping

Welcome to Lesson 8! In this lesson, we'll go shopping. So you'll learn:

☐ the names of stores and common shopping expressions

☐ how to use quantity expressions like **many** and **much**

☐ the names of common articles of **clothing**

☐ how to use the comparative (**bigger**) and the superlative (**biggest**)

☐ how to put it all together in a short conversation about shopping

Ready?

Hello! How Are You?   Big or Small? Short or Tall?   Everyday Life

This Is My Family   Welcome to My Home!

Vocabulary Builder 1

▶ 8A Vocabulary Builder 1 (CD 2, Track 27)

People go to stores to buy things.	
People usually pay with cash or by credit card.	
Mary needs shoes, so she goes to the shoe store.	
John wants a new book, so he goes to the bookstore.	
People buy food at grocery stores or at supermarkets.	
Some people buy bread at a bakery.	
Some people buy meat at a butcher shop.	
Electronics stores sell computers, televisions, and stereos.	
Hardware stores sell paint, hammers, nails, and other things to fix the house.	
Department stores sell all kinds of things, especially clothes.	
Things are cheaper when they're on sale.	
There are a lot of different stores in a mall.	
Many people like to go shopping in malls.	
They spend a lot of money, and a lot of time, in malls.	

Take it Further

▶ 8B Take It Further (CD 2, Track 28)

Did you notice the common verb, spend? You spend money on things.

Houses are expensive, so you spend a lot of money on a new house.	
At Christmas, many people spend a lot of money on gifts.	
We spend two hundred dollars a week on food.	

You also spend time on things.

Mary is a very good student. She spends three hours every night at the library.	
The kids spend too much time watching television!	
We spend two weeks every year in Puerto Rico on vacation.	

✎ Vocabulary Practice 1

▶ 8C Vocabulary Practice 1 (CD 2, Track 29)

Listen to the audio again, and fill in the blanks with the word or words that you hear.

1. People go to stores to _____ things.

2. People usually _____ with cash or by credit card.

3. Mary needs _____ , so she goes to the _____ store.

Hello! How Are You?   Big or Small? Short or Tall?   Everyday Life

This Is My Family   Welcome to My Home!

4. John wants a new_____, so he goes to the _____.

5. People buy food at_____ stores or at

_____.

6. Some people buy bread at a_____.

7. Some people buy meat at a_____ shop.

8. Electronics stores_____ computers, televisions, and stereos.

9. _____ stores sell paint, hammers, nails, and other things to

fix the house.

10. _____ stores sell all kinds of things, especially clothes.

11. Things are_____when they're on sale.

12. There are a lot of different stores in a_____.

13. Many people like to go_____ in malls.

14. They_____ a lot of money, and a lot of time, in malls.

ANSWER KEY

1. **buy**; 2. **pay**; 3. **shoes, shoe**; 4. **book, bookstore**; 5. **grocery, supermarkets**; 6. **bakery**; 7. **butcher**; 8. **sell**; 9. **Hardware**; 10. **Department**; 11. **cheaper**; 12. **mall**; 13. **shopping**; 14. **spend**

Grammar Builder 1

▶ 8D Grammar Builder 1 (CD 2, Track 30)

QUANTITY EXPRESSIONS

To ask about things you count (**one person, two people; one book, three books**), use **how many?**

How many people are there at the store?	

Let's Eat!   At Work   Review Dialogues

Around Town   **Let's Go Shopping**   What Do You Feel Like Doing?

How many stores are there at the mall?	

To ask about things you don't count (money, milk, bread, water, time), use **how much?**

How much money do you spend on food every week?	
How much time do you spend at the store?	

If the answer is zero, use no or not any.

How many people are there at the store? – There are no people at the store. – There aren't any people at the store.	
How much money do you spend on magazines? – I spend no money on magazines. – I don't spend any money on magazines.	

If the answer is a small amount, use a few with things you count (books, people, stores).

You only have ten books? – That's right, I only have a few books.	
There are only three people at the store? – That's right, there are only a few people at the store.	

Hello! How Are You?   Big or Small? Short or Tall?   Everyday Life

This Is My Family   Welcome to My Home!

The mall only has six stores? –That's right, the mall only has a few stores.	

If the answer is a small amount, use a little with things you do not count (money, time, water).

You only spend five dollars on food? –That's right, I only spend a little money on food.	
You only spend fifteen minutes at the store? –That's right, I only spend a little time at the store.	
You only drink one glass of water every day? –That's right, I only drink a little water every day.	

If the answer is a big amount, use a lot of or lots of.

You have five hundred books? –That's right, I have a lot of books. –That's right, I have lots of books.	
You drink fifteen glasses of water a day? –That's right, I drink a lot of water. –That's right, I drink lots of water.	

Much and many also mean a big amount. Use many with things you count, and much with things you do not count.

You have five hundred books? –That's right, I have many books.	

She spends four hours at the library? –Yes, she spends much time at the library.	

Too much and too many mean more than enough.

You have ten cats? You have too many cats!	
You spend ten hours at the mall? You spend too much time shopping!	

Vocabulary Builder 2

▶ 8E Vocabulary Builder 2 (CD 2, Track 31)

John and Mary need new clothes.	
They go shopping at the department store.	
John goes to the men's department.	
He chooses two shirts and a pair of pants.	
He tries the pants on, but they're too big.	
He needs a smaller size.	
He looks at a suit, but it's too expensive.	
He also chooses a jacket and a belt.	
Mary goes to the women's department.	
She chooses a blouse, a pair of pants, and two skirts.	

Hello! How Are You?   Big or Small? Short or Tall?   Everyday Life

This Is My Family   Welcome to My Home!

She tries on the skirts, but she doesn't like them.	
She looks at a dress and a sweater, too.	
The dress is on sale.	
The sweater is cheaper than the dress.	

✎ Vocabulary Practice 2

▶ 8F Vocabulary Practice 2 (CD 3, Track 1)

Listen to your audio again, and fill in the word or words that you hear.

1. John and Mary _____ new clothes.

2. They _____ at the department store.

3. John goes to the men's _____ .

4. He chooses two _____ and a pair of _____ .

5. He tries the pants on, but they're _____ .

6. He needs a _____ size.

7. He looks at a suit, but it's _____ .

8. He also chooses a _____ and a _____ .

9. Mary goes to the _____ .

10. She chooses a _____ , a pair of pants, and two _____ .

11. She _____ on the skirts, but she doesn't like them.

12. She looks at a _____ and a _____ , too.

13. The dress is _____.

14. The sweater is _____ than the dress.

ANSWER KEY
1. need; 2. go shopping; 3. department; 4. shirts, pants; 5. too big; 6. smaller; 7. too expensive; 8. jacket, belt; 9. women's department; 10. blouse, skirts; 11. tries; 12. dress, sweater; 13. on sale; 14. cheaper

Grammar Builder 2
▶ 8G Grammar Builder 2 (CD 3, Track 2)

THE COMPARATIVE (BIGGER) AND THE SUPERLATIVE (BIGGEST)

To compare two people or things, add –er to the adjective: old – older; young – younger.

John is twenty-three years old, and Mary is twenty five.	
Mary is older than John.	
John is younger than Mary.	

Some adjectives double the last consonant: big – bigger; hot – hotter.

California is bigger than New Jersey.	
Miami is hotter than Boston.	

If an adjective ends in –y, y becomes i before –er: easy – easier; happy – happier.

Algebra is easier than calculus.	
Susan is happier than Jeff.	

Hello! How Are You?   Big or Small? Short or Tall?   Everyday Life

This Is My Family   Welcome to My Home!

Long adjectives use **more** instead of **–er**: **difficult – more difficult; expensive – more expensive; beautiful – more beautiful.**

Calculus is more difficult than algebra.	
A suit is more expensive than a shirt.	
Is San Francisco more beautiful than Los Angeles?	

To compare three or more people or things, add **–est** to the adjective: **big – bigger – biggest; tall – taller – tallest.**

Alaska is the biggest state in the United States.	
Mount Everest is the tallest mountain in the world.	

If an adjective uses **more** instead of **–er**, it also uses **most** instead of **–est.**

This is the most expensive computer in the store.	
What is the most beautiful city in the world?	

Some common adjectives are irregular: **good – better – best; bad – worse – worst.**

Mary is a better student than Peter, but Sam is the best student in the class.	
This is the cheapest computer in the store, but it's also the worst.	

The opposite of more is less, and the opposite of the most is the least.

The red shirt costs fifty dollars, and the blue shirt costs forty dollars, so the blue shirt is less expensive than the red shirt.	
The green shirt costs thirty dollars; it's the least expensive shirt.	

Finally, remember that too means more than enough.

I need a size 10 shoe. This is a size 9; it's too small.	
That shirt is one hundred dollars? That's too expensive!	

✎ Work Out 1

▶ 8H Work Out 1 (CD 3, Track 3)

Listen and write the words you hear.

1. Russia is the _____ country in the world.

2. Is your computer _____ than my computer?

3. This shirt is _____ small; I need a _____ size.

4. The Thai restaurant is _____ than the Italian restaurant.

5. Is a dress _____ than a skirt?

6. Who is the _____ professor at the university?

7. Today is the _____ day of the year.

8. This is the _____ class!

Hello! How Are You?   Big or Small? Short or Tall?   Everyday Life

This Is My Family   Welcome to My Home!

9. Clothes in this store are _____ than clothes at the mall.

10. They live in the _____ house on the street.

11. My car is _____ than your car.

12. That is the _____ book in the library!

ANSWER KEY

1. biggest; 2. newer; 3. too, bigger; 4. better; 5. more expensive; 6. best; 7. longest; 8. most difficult; 9. cheaper; 10. smallest; 11. less expensive; 12. least interesting

🔊 Bring It All Together

▶ 81 Bring It All Together (CD 3, Track 4)

Jack and Melissa are shopping for clothes. Listen in.

Jack:	What do you think about this blue shirt?
Melissa:	Not bad … It's better than the red shirt.
Jack:	Yeah, but it's more expensive, too.
Melissa:	Well, better clothes cost more.
Jack:	Oh, come on. That's not true. Some cheap clothes are good.
Melissa:	Not many! But the blue shirt is nice. It's the nicest shirt in the store.
Jack:	Great. I'll get it. But I need a pair of pants, too.
Melissa:	Do you want jeans? They sell really great jeans here.
Jack:	Not jeans; something less casual. I need them for work.
Melissa:	Here. How about these gray pants?
Jack:	They're nice! What size are they?
Melissa:	Thirty-one.
Jack:	That's too small. I wear thirty-two.
Melissa:	Ah, here we go. Size thirty-two.
Jack:	But how much do they cost?
Melissa:	I don't know. I don't see any price tag. Oh, here it is. Sixty dollars. And look, they're on sale. Twenty percent off!

Jack:	That's not bad! Forty dollars!
Melissa:	Forty dollars? You mean forty-eight dollars. I hope your cooking is better than your math.
Jack:	Oops, yeah. My math is much worse than my cooking. Why?
Melissa:	Because I'm hungry, and you're cooking dinner tonight.

✎ Work Out 2

Choose the correct word.

1. How (much/many) shirts do you have?

2. They only have a (little/few) money.

3. There aren't (some/any) good clothing stores at the mall.

4. We have a (little/few) pairs of pants in size thirty-two.

5. You eat too (much/many) sugar!

6. There are (much/many) good restaurants in the city.

7. We don't have (some/any) more blouses in your size.

8. How (much/many) water do you drink every day?

9. They have (some/any) nice belts in the men's department.

10. We don't have (much/many) time for shopping today.

ANSWER KEY
1. many; 2. little; 3. any; 4. few; 5. much; 6. many; 7. any; 8. much; 9. some; 10. much

Hello! How Are You?　　　　　Big or Small? Short or Tall?　　　　　Everyday Life

This Is My Family　　　　　Welcome to My Home!

Choose the correct adjective.

1. Billy is the _____ boy in the class.

    a. taller

    b. tallest

    c. most tall

    d. more tall

2. Is the Nile _____ than the Amazon?

    a. longest

    b. long

    c. most long

    d. longer

3. This belt is _____ than the shirt.

    a. more expensive

    b. most expensive

    c. the most expensive

    d. expensive

4. This is the _____ clothing store in the mall.

    a. good

    b. better

    c. most good

    d. best

5. I need a _____ computer.

   a. faster

   b. most fast

   c. fastest

   d. more fast

6. The dress is very _____.

   a. more beautiful

   b. less beautiful

   c. beautiful

   d. most beautiful

7. Do you have a _____ size?

   a. smallest

   b. smaller

   c. least small

   d. more small

8. Who is_____, Jack or Dan?

   a. old

   b. oldest

   c. more old

   d. older

Hello! How Are You?   Big or Small? Short or Tall?   Everyday Life

This Is My Family   Welcome to My Home!

9. Her question is very _____.

   a. **more difficult**

   b. **most difficult**

   c. **difficult**

   d. **the most difficult**

10. This is the _____ pair of pants in the store.

   a. **cheap**

   b. **more cheap**

   c. **cheaper**

   d. **cheapest**

   ANSWER KEY
   1. b; 2. d; 3. a; 4. d; 5. a; 6. c; 7. b; 8. d; 9. c; 10. d

✎ Drive It Home

Let's practice **much**, **many**, and other quantity expressions. First, ask:

How much … is there? or **How many … are there?**

1. coffee

   _____

2. shoes

   _____

3. electronics stores

   _____

Let's Eat! At Work Review Dialogues

Around Town **Let's Go Shopping** What Do You Feel Like Doing?

4. time

_____

5. sugar

_____

6. people

_____

7. shirts

_____

8. money

_____

9. pairs of pants

_____

10. water

_____

ANSWER KEY

1. How much coffee is there? 2. How many shoes are there? 3. How many electronics stores are there? 4. How much time is there? 5. How much sugar is there? 6. How many people are there? 7. How many shirts are there? 8. How much money is there? 9. How many pairs of pants are there? 10. How much water is there?

Hello! How Are You?   Big or Small? Short or Tall?   Everyday Life

This Is My Family   Welcome to My Home!

Now say:

There is a little ... or **There are a few ...**

1. milk

   _____

2. skirts

   _____

3. forks

   _____

4. food

   _____

5. students

   _____

6. clothing stores

   _____

7. time

   _____

8. belts

   _____

9. coffee

10. pairs of shoes

ANSWER KEY

1. There is a little milk. 2. There are a few skirts. 3. There are a few forks. 4. There is a little food. 5. There are a few students. 6. There are a few clothing stores. 7. There is a little time. 8. There are a few belts. 9. There is a little coffee. 10. There are a few pairs of shoes.

Parting Words

Congratulations! You finished Lesson 8. Do you know:

☐ the names of stores and common shopping expressions? (No? Go back to 164.)

☐ how to use quantity expressions like **many** and **much**? (No? Go back to 166.)

☐ the names of common articles of **clothing**? (No? Go back to 169.)

☐ how to use the comparative (**bigger**) and the superlative (**biggest**)? (No? Go back to 171.)

☐ how to put it all together in a short conversation about shopping? (No? Go back to 174.)

Don't forget to practice and reinforce what you've learned by visiting www.livinglanguage.com/languagelab for flashcards, games, and quizzes!

Hello! How Are You?   Big or Small? Short or Tall?   Everyday Life

This Is My Family   Welcome to My Home!

Word Recall

Do you remember the vocabulary from Lesson 8?

A.

1. What do people usually do at stores?

_____

2. If you don't have cash, you can pay by ...

_____

3. Where do you buy shoes?

_____

4. Where do you buy books?

_____

5. Where do you buy food?

_____

6. Where do some people buy bread and cakes?

_____

7. Where do some people buy meat?

_____

8. What kind of store sells computers, televisions, and stereos?

_____

Let's Eat!   At Work   Review Dialogues

Around Town   **Let's Go Shopping**   What Do You Feel Like Doing?

9. What kind of store sells paint, hammers, nails, and other things to fix the house?

_____

10. Are things cheaper or more expensive when they're on sale?

_____

11. What do you call a place with a lot of different stores?

_____

B.

1. If a pair of pants is too big, you need a _____ size.

2. If a sweater is too expensive, you need something _____ .

3. Before you buy new clothes, you try them _____ .

ANSWER KEY:
A. 1. They buy things. They go shopping. 2. credit card; 3. at a shoe store; 4. at a bookstore;
5. at a supermarket or grocery store; 6. at a bakery (or supermarket); 7. at a butcher shop (or
supermarket); 8. an electronics store (or department store); 9. hardware store; 10. They're
cheaper. 11. a mall

B. 1. smaller; 2. cheaper (or less expensive); 3. on

Hello! How Are You?   Big or Small? Short or Tall?   Everyday Life

This Is My Family   Welcome to My Home!

Lesson 9:
At Work

Hello! This lesson is about work, so you'll learn:

☐ the names of common jobs and professions

☐ how to use want to, have to, can, must, should, and need to

☐ important vocabulary to talk about work and offices

☐ how to use is working, am going, are taking, and so on

☐ how to put it all together in a conversation at the office

Let's get started with some new vocabulary.

Vocabulary Builder 1

▶ 9A Vocabulary Builder 1 (CD 3, Track 5)

A teacher works in a school and teaches students.	
A professor works at a university and teaches students.	
A doctor works at a hospital and treats sick people.	
A nurse also works at a hospital and helps doctors and sick people.	
A lawyer works at a law firm and practices law.	
A plumber comes to your house and repairs the sink or toilet.	
An architect designs houses and office buildings.	
A construction worker builds houses and other buildings.	
An engineer designs bridges, highways, and other big projects.	
A carpenter works with wood and makes tables, chairs, cabinets, and other things.	
A factory worker works in a factory and makes cars or other products.	
A mail carrier delivers your mail.	
A salesperson works in a store and sells things.	

Hello! How Are You?   Big or Small? Short or Tall?   Everyday Life

This Is My Family   Welcome to My Home!

A cook works in a restaurant and prepares food.	
An office manager organizes an office.	
A secretary answers the phone in an office, writes reports, and does many other things.	
A police officer protects people and fights crime.	
A fire fighter puts out fires.	

✎ Vocabulary Practice 1

Match the job in the left column with the work description in the right.

1. A teacher ...

2. A nurse ...

3. A lawyer ...

4. An engineer ...

5. A plumber ...

6. A mail carrier ...

7. An architect ...

8. A construction worker ...

a. designs bridges, highways, and other big projects.

b. works with wood and makes tables, chairs, cabinets, and other things.

c. works at a hospital and treats sick people.

d. answers the phone in an office, writes reports, and does many other things.

e. works at a university and teaches students.

f. works at a hospital and helps doctors and sick people.

g. protects people and fights crime.

h. comes to your house and repairs the sink or toilet.

9. A carpenter ...   i. works in a store and sells things.

10. A secretary ...   j. works at a law firm and practices law.

11. A doctor ...   k. builds houses and other buildings.

12. A factory worker ...   l. puts out fires.

13. A salesperson ...   m. designs houses and office buildings.

14. A professor ...   n. organizes an office.

15. A cook ...   o. works in a school and teaches students.

16. An office manager ...   p. works in a restaurant and prepares food.

17. A fire fighter ...   q. works in a factory and makes cars or other products.

18. A police officer ...   r. delivers your mail.

ANSWER KEY

1. o; 2. f; 3. j; 4. a; 5. h; 6. r; 7. m; 8. k; 9. b; 10. d; 11. c; 12. q; 13. i; 14. e; 15. p; 16. n; 17. l; 18. g

Grammar Builder 1

▶ 9B Grammar Builder 1 (CD 3, Track 6)

THE VERBS WANT TO, HAVE TO, CAN, MUST, SHOULD, AND NEED TO

Use the verbs want to, have to, can, must, should, and need to with another verb: want to eat, have to study, can speak, should drink, needs to go, etc.

Use want to to express a desire. The he/she/it form of want to is wants to. The negative is don't want to or doesn't want to.

| I'm hungry. I want to eat. | |
| Bill doesn't like his job. He wants to get a new job. | |

Hello! How Are You?   Big or Small? Short or Tall?   Everyday Life

This Is My Family   Welcome to My Home!

| We don't like pizza. We don't want to eat pizza. | |

Use **can** to express ability. There is no –s on **can** in the **he/she/it** form. The negative of **can** is **can't** or **cannot**.

George knows English, Japanese, and Russian. He can speak three languages.	
I don't speak Chinese, so I can't understand Li.	
We don't have any money, so we cannot buy a new car.	

Use **have to** to express necessity or obligation. The **he/she/it** form is **has to**. The negative is **don't have to** or **doesn't have to**.

It's eight thirty; I have to leave for work.	
Barbara has a test tomorrow; she has to study tonight.	
Tomorrow is Saturday, so we don't have to work.	

Must is similar to **have to**, but it's more formal or urgent. There is no –s on **must** in the **he/she/it** form.

| It's eight thirty. I must leave for work. | |
| Barbara has a test tomorrow; she must study tonight. | |

Must not is not the same as **don't/doesn't have to.**

It's Saturday. You don't have to go to work today. You can stay home.	
You're sick! You must not go to work today! You have to stay home.	

Use **should** to express a suggestion. There is no –s on the **he/she/it** form. The negative is **shouldn't.**

You don't drink enough water. You should drink more water.	
It's late and we have to work tomorrow. We should go home now.	
You shouldn't smoke! It's bad for you.	

Use **need to** to express necessity or obligation. The **he/she/it** form is **needs to.** The negative is **don't need to** or **doesn't need to.**

My computer doesn't work. I need to buy a new computer.	
I have a test tomorrow. I need to study.	
You don't need to pay with cash. You can pay with your credit card.	

In questions, **can, must,** and **should** come before the subject.

Can you speak Polish?	
How many languages can you speak?	
Why must you speak with her secretary?	

Hello! How Are You?   Big or Small? Short or Tall?   Everyday Life

This Is My Family   Welcome to My Home!

Should we stay home or go to a restaurant?	

Use do or does with want to, have to, and need to.

Do you want to go to the library with me tomorrow?	
Does Mary have to work next week?	
Do I need to pay with cash, or can I use my credit card?	

Vocabulary Builder 2

▶ 9C Vocabulary Builder 2 (CD 3, Track 7)

Jack works in an office.	
He works from nine o'clock to five o'clock, from Monday to Friday.	
He works for Gloria Peterson; she is his boss.	
Jack is Gloria's assistant.	
He answers her phone and takes messages when she isn't in her office.	
He organizes her meetings.	
When someone wants to see her, he schedules an appointment.	
He updates her calendar with new meetings.	
Jack works on his computer most of the time.	

He sends e-mails, writes reports, and makes photocopies.	
Jack has a lunch break at twelve thirty every day.	
It's twelve forty now, so Jack is not working.	
He is eating lunch with his coworkers.	

✎ Vocabulary Practice 2

▶ 9D Vocabulary Practice 2 (CD 3, Track 8)

Let's practice the new vocabulary. Listen to your audio again, and fill in the missing word or words.

1. Jack _____ in an office.

2. He works _____ nine o'clock to five o'clock, from Monday _____ Friday.

3. He works _____ Gloria Peterson; she is his _____.

4. Jack is Gloria's _____.

5. He _____ her phone and takes _____ when she isn't in her office.

6. He organizes her _____.

7. When someone wants to see her, he _____ an

_____.

Hello! How Are You? Big or Small? Short or Tall? Everyday Life

This Is My Family Welcome to My Home!

8. He updates her _____ with new meetings.

9. Jack works _____ his computer _____ of the time.

10. He _____ e-mails, _____ reports,

and _____ photocopies.

11. Jack has a lunch break at twelve thirty _____ day.

12. It's twelve forty _____, so Jack is not _____.

13. He is _____ lunch with his coworkers.

ANSWER KEY

1. works; 2. from, to; 3. for, boss; 4. assistant; 5. answers, messages; 6. meetings; 7. schedules, appointment; 8. calendar; 9. on, most; 10. sends; writes, makes; 11. every; 12. now, working; 13. eating

Grammar Builder 2

▶ 9E Grammar Builder 2 (CD 3, Track 9)

THE PRESENT PROGRESSIVE:
IS WORKING, AM GOING, ARE TAKING

You learned the simple present in Lesson 5: **I work, you work, he works, she works**, etc. You use the simple present with time expressions like **usually, on Tuesdays, at nine o'clock, every day, in the afternoons, always, generally, never**, and so on.

Jack works on Mondays, Tuesdays, Wednesdays, Thursdays, and Fridays.	
Jack never works on Saturday or Sunday.	
He usually gets to work at nine o'clock.	

But sometimes he gets to work at eight thirty.	
He always eats lunch at twelve thirty.	

But you use the present progressive (–ing) to express something that is happening now.

Today is Monday, so Jack is working.	
Today is Saturday, so Jack is not working.	
It's nine o'clock, so Jack is walking into the office.	
It's twelve thirty, so Jack is eating lunch.	

The present progressive is formed with be (am, is, are) + the verb + –ing.

I am working	we are working
you are working	you are working
he/she/it is working	they are working

In the negative, put not before the verb.

I am not eating	we are not eating
you are not eating	you are not eating
he/she/it is not eating	they are not eating

Hello! How Are You?   Big or Small? Short or Tall?   Everyday Life

This Is My Family   Welcome to My Home!

Don't forget the other forms of be in the negative: **you're not/you aren't, he's not/he isn't**, etc.

I'm not sleeping	we're not sleeping/we aren't sleeping
you're not sleeping/you aren't sleeping	you're not sleeping/you aren't sleeping
he's not sleeping/he isn't sleeping she's not sleeping/she isn't sleeping	they're not sleeping/they aren't sleeping

In questions, **am**, **is**, or **are** comes before the subject.

Are you working now?	
Is she eating lunch with her coworkers?	
What is he saying? I can't hear.	

The present progressive is also used to express events in the future, with expressions like **tonight, tomorrow, next week**, and so on.

We're going to a new restaurant tonight.	
Are you working tomorrow, or do you have the day off?	
They're meeting next week.	

Finally, there are a few spelling changes in the present progressive. If a verb ends in –e, there is no –e before –ing: **come – coming; take – taking**. Many verbs that end in a single consonant double the consonant before –ing: **get – getting; put – putting**. And if a verb ends in –ie, change –ie to –y before –ing: **lie – lying; die – dying**. But keep y if the verb ends in y: **try – trying; copy – copying**.

✎ Work Out 1

▷ 9F Work Out 1 (CD 3, Track 10)

Listen to your audio, and write the word or words you hear.

1. We _____ speak with your boss.

2. Does he _____ go to work tomorrow morning?

3. What _____ I say to Mrs. Jenson?

4. We _____ finish the report today.

5. _____ you understand the question?

6. You're sick; you _____ to work today.

7. Bill _____ a new job soon.

8. She _____ the telephone.

9. You _____ jeans to the office.

10. Where _____ work?

ANSWER KEY
1. want to; 2. have to; 3. should; 4. don't have to; 5. Can; 6. must not go; 7. needs to find; 8. can't hear;
9. shouldn't wear; 10. do you want to

ᴬᴬ Bring It All Together

▷ 9G Bring It All Together (CD 3, Track 11)

Mark and Sue work at the same company. They meet at the office. Listen in.

Mark:	Hey, Sue! What are you doing?
Sue:	I'm finishing a report for my boss. What are you doing?
Mark:	I'm leaving for lunch. Do you want to come?
Sue:	Oh, sorry. I can't leave right now.

Hello! How Are You?   Big or Small? Short or Tall?   Everyday Life

This Is My Family   Welcome to My Home!

Mark: Why not? It's twelve thirty.

Sue: Yeah, but I'm going to a meeting in ten minutes.

Mark: Oh, too bad. Don't you usually have lunch at twelve thirty?

Sue: Yes, I usually eat at twelve thirty, but today I have an important meeting. So I have to stay at the office and eat later.

Mark: Well, what are you doing tonight after work?

Sue: Tonight? I have to work until six, but I don't have any plans after that. Why? What's going on?

Mark: It's Bill's birthday, so a few of us are going to dinner. You should come.

Sue: Today's Bill's birthday? I want to come, but I have to come into the office early tomorrow. My boss needs to have my report by nine, so I'll need to work on it tomorrow morning.

Mark: No problem. We're having dinner at seven. So you can be home by eleven.

Sue: Eleven? That's a long dinner! You're eating from seven until eleven?

Mark: No. After dinner we're probably seeing a movie. But you don't have to come to the movies if you need to get home early.

Sue: That sounds good. I can meet all of you for dinner, but I should leave by eight thirty.

Mark: Perfect. After lunch, look for an e-mail from me with the address of the restaurant.

Sue: Okay. Have a great lunch, and I'll see you later tonight.

✎ Work Out 2

Let's practice want to, have to, can, must, should, and need to. Choose the correct answer.

1. Greg speaks Spanish and English. He (should/can) speak two languages.

2. It's late and I'm working tomorrow. I (can/need to) get home.

3. You don't eat enough vegetables. You (**want to/should**) eat more vegetables.

4. Tomorrow is Saturday and I'm not working, so I (**don't have to/must not**) get home early tonight.

5. Julia's car is old and ugly. She (**wantsto/can**) buy a new car.

6. We don't have very much money, so we (**don't want to/can't**) go to an expensive restaurant.

7. It's eight thirty and Bill starts work at nine o'clock. He (**wants to/has to**) leave for work.

8. It's cold outside! You (**don'thave to/must not**) go outside without a jacket.

9. The music is too loud. We (**can't/shouldn't**) hear you.

10. Carla doesn't like her job. She (**can/wants to**) find a new one.

ANSWER KEY

1. can; 2. need to; 3. should; 4. don't have to; 5. wants to; 6. can't; 7. has to; 8. must not; 9. can't; 10. wants to

Great. Now choose the correct verb tense, either simple present or present progressive.

1. They (**watch/are watching**) television right now.

2. I usually (**get/am getting**) to work at eight forty-five in the morning.

3. Doctors (**work/are working**) in hospitals.

4. The nurse (**helps/is helping**) the doctor with a patient now.

5. What (**do you do/are you doing**) later tonight?

6. Where (**do they go/are they going**) for vacation every year?

Hello! How Are You?   Big or Small? Short or Tall?   Everyday Life

This Is My Family   Welcome to My Home!

7. The plumber (**doesn't work/isn't working**) on Sundays.

8. Who (**goes/is going**) to the movies with you this weekend?

9. I can't hear. What (**do they say/are they saying**)?

10. My father (**goes/is going**) to the office sometimes on Saturday mornings.

ANSWER KEY
1. are watching; 2. get; 3. work; 4. is helping; 5. are you doing; 6. do they go; 7. doesn't work; 8. is going; 9. are they saying; 10. goes

✎ Drive It Home

Change each sentence from the simple present to the present progressive.

Example: I drink a cup of coffee.
Answer: **I'm drinking a cup of coffee.**

1. The plumber comes to their house.

   _____

2. We eat dinner at a Japanese restaurant.

   _____

3. They speak to their bosses.

   _____

4. The kids sleep in their bedroom.

   _____

5. I have breakfast with my family.

   _____

6. The engineer designs a bridge.

7. The salesperson helps the customer.

8. The construction workers build an apartment building.

ANSWER KEY

1. The plumber is coming to their house. 2. We're eating dinner at a Japanese restaurant. 3. They're speaking to their bosses. 4. The kids are sleeping in their bedroom. 5. I'm having breakfast with my family. 6. The engineer is designing a bridge. 7. The salesperson is helping the customer. 8. The construction workers are building an apartment building.

Parting Words

Terrific! You finished Lesson 9. That means that there's only one more lesson in Essential English. Do you know:

☐ the names of common jobs and professions? (No? Go back to 185.)

☐ how to use **want to, have to, can, must, should,** and **need to?** (No? Go back to 187.)

☐ important vocabulary to talk about work and offices? (No? Go back to 190.)

☐ how to use **is working, am going, are taking,** and so on? (No? Go back to 192.)

☐ how to put it all together in a conversation at the office? (No? Go back to 195.)

Don't forget to practice and reinforce what you've learned by visiting www.livinglanguage.com/languagelab for flashcards, games, and quizzes!

Hello! How Are You? Big or Small? Short or Tall? Everyday Life

This Is My Family Welcome to My Home!

Word Recall

Let's review jobs and professions.

1. Who works in a school with students? _____

2. Who teaches at a university? _____

3. Who comes to your house and repairs the sink or toilet? _____

4. Who protects people and fights crime? _____

5. Who works at a hospital and treats sick people? _____

6. Who delivers your mail? _____

7. Who works with wood and makes tables, chairs, and cabinets? _____

8. Who works at a law firm and practices law? _____

9. Who works in a restaurant and prepares food? _____

10. Who designs houses and office buildings? _____

11. Who answers the phone in an office and writes reports? _____

12. Who builds houses and other buildings? _____

13. Who works in a hospital and helps doctors and sick people? _____

14. Who puts out fires? _____

15. Who works in a store and sells things? _____

16. Who organizes an office? _____

17. Who designs bridges, highways, and other big projects? _____

18. Who works in a factory and makes cars or other products? _____

ANSWER KEY
1. a teacher; 2. a professor; 3. a plumber; 4. a police officer; 5. a doctor; 6. a mail carrier; 7. a
carpenter; 8. a lawyer; 9. a cook; 10. an architect; 11. a secretary (or an assistant); 12. a construction
worker; 13. a nurse; 14. a fire fighter; 15. a sales person; 16. an office manager; 17. an engineer;
18. a factory worker

Hello! How Are You?   Big or Small? Short or Tall?   Everyday Life

This Is My Family   Welcome to My Home!

Lesson 10:
What Do You Feel Like Doing?

Hi there! This is your last lesson of *Essential English*. Congratulations! This lesson is about your hobbies, interests, and free time. You'll learn:

☐ vocabulary for hobbies and interests

☐ how to talk about what you **like** and what you **don't like**

☐ vocabulary for free time activities

☐ how to use demonstratives like **this** and **that**

☐ how to put it all together in a conversation about weekend plans

Let's get started.

Vocabulary Builder 1

▶ 10A Vocabulary Builder 1 (CD 3, Track 12)

What are your hobbies?	
I like cooking and reading.	
I like to go horseback riding.	
We love to go hiking in the mountains.	
We also like to go camping.	
Bill loves to bike.	
Sue likes to go running.	
Greg loves to play guitar, but Diane prefers to play piano.	
Nicole enjoys sewing.	
Do you like collecting stamps or coins?	
My parents like to take long walks.	
Eddie likes to draw.	
We enjoy boating during the summer.	

✎ Vocabulary Practice 1

▶ 10B Vocabulary Practice 1 (CD 3, Track 13)

Listen to the audio again, and fill in the missing word or words.

1. What are your _____ ?

2. I like _____ and _____ .

3. I like _____ horseback riding.

Hello! How Are You?　　　Big or Small? Short or Tall?　　　Everyday Life

This Is My Family　　　Welcome to My Home!

4. We _____ to go hiking in the mountains.

5. We also like to _____.

6. Bill loves _____.

7. Sue likes to _____.

8. Greg loves to _____ guitar, but Diane _____ to play piano.

9. Nicole _____ sewing.

10. Do you like _____ stamps or coins?

11. My parents like to _____ long _____.

12. Eddie likes _____.

13. We enjoy_____ during the summer.

ANSWER KEY

1. hobbies; 2. cooking, reading; 3. to go; 4. love; 5. go camping; 6. to bike; 7. go running; 8. play, prefers; 9. enjoys; 10. collecting; 11. take, walks; 12. to draw; 13. boating

Grammar Builder 1

▶ 10C Grammar Builder 1 (CD 3, Track 14)

TALKING ABOUT WHAT YOU LIKE

Like is a common verb in English. You can **like** a person or thing:

I'm happy at my new job; I like my new boss a lot.	
I want to go to a Thai restaurant, because I like Thai food.	

You can also use like with a verb, either in its to-infinitive form (to go, to cook, to read), or its –ing form (going, cooking, reading).

I like to go to the library. I like going to the library.	
Pete likes cooking. Pete likes to cook.	
We like to read. We like reading.	

You can use a lot, really, or very much with like.

My niece likes to go horseback riding a lot.	
John really likes collecting stamps.	
My family likes to go boating very much.	

In the negative, use do/does not.

We don't like to sew. We don't like sewing.	
She doesn't like to cook. She doesn't like cooking.	

The verb enjoy means the same thing as like, but it is only used with the –ing form of a verb.

Sarah enjoys reading the newspaper on Sunday mornings.	
We enjoy having dinner with our friends.	

Hello! How Are You?   Big or Small? Short or Tall?   Everyday Life

This Is My Family   Welcome to My Home!

Love means to like very, very much. You can love a person or a thing, you can **love to do** something, or you can **love doing** something.

John loves his wife very much.	
Mary loves her children.	
I love sushi! Let's go to a Japanese restaurant.	
We love relaxing and reading books on the weekends. We love to relax and read books on the weekends.	

The verb **prefer** means **to like more**.

I like watching television, but I prefer to read.	
We like camping, but we prefer going to the beach.	

If you don't like something very, very much, you **hate** it. Use **hate** with things, or verbs in the **to**-infinitive form or the **–ing** form.

I hate sushi! I don't want to go to a Japanese restaurant.	
The kids hate studying. The kids hate to study.	

Another expression that means **doesn't like** is **can't stand**. It is used with people, things, or verbs in the **–ing** form.

Sheila can't stand her new boss.	
Bob can't stand watching television.	

Vocabulary Builder 2

▶ 10D Vocabulary Builder 2 (CD 3, Track 15)

What do you feel like doing tonight?	
I feel like seeing a movie.	
What's playing at the movies?	
There's a romantic comedy, an action film, and a horror film.	
I don't feel like seeing a horror film; let's see the romantic comedy.	
We want to get together with friends at a restaurant.	
We're inviting friends to our place for a dinner party.	
John feels like seeing a play.	
Do you prefer the theater or the opera?	
Bill can't stand the opera!	
Josh wants to get together with friends this weekend to watch the football game.	
I can't stand football; I prefer baseball.	
George doesn't play baseball, but he plays basketball.	
I love soccer. It's a lot of fun!	
I can't stand soccer! It's boring.	
No, it's not. Soccer is exciting!	

Hello! How Are You?   Big or Small? Short or Tall?   Everyday Life

This Is My Family   Welcome to My Home!

| Let's play cards tonight. | |
| No, I feel like playing chess. | |

Take It Further

▶ 10E Take It Further (CD 3, Track 16)

Notice the expression feel like. It means want (to).

| What do you want to do tonight?
What do you feel like doing tonight? | |
| What do you feel like eating?
I feel like pizza. | |

You saw the verb play used with musical instruments or with movies.

| Greg loves to play guitar, but Diane prefers to play piano. | |
| What's playing at the movies?
A romantic comedy is playing. | |

Play is also used with sports.

Paul loves to play basketball.	
John prefers to play football.	
Do you like playing tennis?	
The high school students are playing football.	
Do you prefer to play football or soccer?	

Notice that in the United States, football means (American) football, and soccer is the sport that's called football in most other countries.

To play is also used with games, for example, **cards** or **chess**.

Let's play cards tonight.	
No, I feel like playing chess.	

You can also use **play** generally, as in:

The dog is playing with the cat.	
The kids are playing outside.	

Finally, you see **a play** at the theater.

Let's go to the theater and see a play.	

✎ Vocabulary Practice 2

▶ 10F Vocabulary Practice 2 (CD 3, Track 17)

Listen to the audio and write the missing word or words.

1. What do you _____ tonight?

2. I feel like _____ a movie.

3. What's _____ at the movies?

4. There's a romantic _____, an _____ film, and a _____ film.

5. I _____ seeing a horror film; let's see the romantic comedy.

6. We want to get _____ with friends at a restaurant.

7. We're _____ friends to our place for a dinner _____.

Hello! How Are You?   Big or Small? Short or Tall?   Everyday Life

This Is My Family   Welcome to My Home!

8. John feels like seeing a _____.

9. Do you prefer the _____ or the _____?

10. Bill _____ the opera!

11. Josh wants to _____ with friends this weekend to

watch the football _____.

12. I can't stand _____; I prefer _____.

13. George doesn't _____ baseball, but he _____ basketball.

14. I _____ soccer. It's a lot of _____!

15. I can't stand soccer! It's _____!

16. No it's not. Soccer is _____!

17. Let's play _____ tonight.

18. No, I feel like playing _____.

ANSWER KEY

1. feel like doing; 2. seeing; 3. playing; 4. comedy, action, horror; 5. don't feel like; 6. together;
7. inviting, party; 8. play; 9. theater, opera; 10. can't stand; 11. get together, game; 12. football,
baseball; 13. play, plays; 14. love, fun; 15. boring; 16. exciting; 17. cards; 18. chess

Grammar Builder 2

▶ 10G Grammar Builder 2 (CD 3, Track 18)

DEMONSTRATIVES: THIS AND THAT

Use **this** with singular things that are near you. Use **these** with plural things that
are near you.

This book is really interesting.	
These pants are very expensive.	

Use **that** with singular things that are not near you. Use **those** with plural things that are not near you.

| That restaurant in the mall is not very good. | |
| Those people in the park are playing soccer. | |

Use **this, that, these,** and **those** with a noun (**book, pants, restaurant, people**), or use them alone.

| Do you like that? No, I prefer this. | |
| Are these your books? Yes, those are my books. | |

You can also say **this one** and **that one.**

| That one is nice, but I prefer this one. | |
| I like this one, but that one is nicer. | |

✎ Work Out 1

▶ 10H Work Out 1 (CD 3, Track 19)

Listen and write the word or words you hear.

1. Do you like _____ chess?

2. No, I _____ playing chess. I _____ cards.

3. Do you _____ a romantic comedy?

4. No, I _____ romantic comedies! _____ see an action film.

Hello! How Are You?   Big or Small? Short or Tall?   Everyday Life

This Is My Family   Welcome to My Home!

5. They _____ to go camping.

6. I prefer to _____ home and _____.

7. Do you feel like _____ to a restaurant tonight?

8. Yes, let's go out. I _____ cooking.

9. Do you _____ collecting stamps?

10. No, collecting stamps is _____.

ANSWER KEY
1. playing; 2. can't stand, prefer; 3. feel like seeing; 4. hate, Let's; 5. really like; 6. stay, read;
7. going out; 8. don't feel like; 9. enjoy; 10. boring

Bring It All Together
▶ 101 Bring It All Together (CD 3, Track 20)

Jen and Rob are discussing their weekend plans. Listen in.

Jen:	What do you feel like doing this weekend?
Rob:	Nothing! I'm tired. I want to stay home and relax.
Jen:	Oh, come on. Let's do something. Ed and Sarah are having a dinner party on Saturday night.
Rob:	Ed and Sarah? You know I can't stand their food. They cook horrible food.
Jen:	Come on. They're our friends, and they're inviting us to dinner. Just one night.
Rob:	Well, I can have a big lunch and eat something before we go.
Jen:	Perfect. So, Saturday night we're visiting friends for dinner. What about Sunday?
Rob:	There's a football game on Sunday. I want to watch it.
Jen:	You want to spend your Sunday sitting in front of the television and watching a football game?
Rob:	Yes.

Jen:	That's boring!
Rob:	No, football games are exciting!
Jen:	Playing football is exciting, but sitting around watching television is boring.
Ron:	Well, what do you want to do?
Jen:	The weather is nice. Let's go hiking.
Ron:	Nah, I don't like hiking.
Jen:	How about biking? We have new bikes.
Rob:	Yeah, that's true. And they're expensive. We should use them.
Jen:	Perfect, so tomorrow we're having dinner with friends, and on Sunday we're going biking. A wonderful weekend.
Rob:	Okay, but Monday I'm staying in and watching television.

✎ Work Out 2

Let's practice likes and dislikes. Answer each question, following the cues.

Example: Do you like playing tennis? (Yes, very much.)
Answer: **Yes, I like playing tennis very much.**

1. Do you like watching basketball games? (Yes.)

   _____

2. Does Bill like going camping? (No.)

   _____

3. Do you like horseback riding. (Yes, very much.)

   _____

4. Does Mary like cooking? (No, hates.)

   _____

Hello! How Are You?   Big or Small? Short or Tall?   Everyday Life

This Is My Family   Welcome to My Home!

5. Do the kids like doing homework? (No, can't stand.)

_____

6. Does Jack like going to the movies? (Yes, loves.)

_____

7. Does Marta like the opera? (Yes, but prefers the theater.)

_____

8. Do you enjoy watching soccer on television? (Yes, but prefer playing.)

_____

9. Does Paul like to play chess? (No, not very much.)

_____

10. Does Sam like inviting friends over for dinner? (Yes, loves.)

_____

ANSWER KEY
1. Yes, I like watching basketball games. 2. No, Bill doesn't like going camping. 3. Yes, I like horseback riding very much. 4. No, Mary hates cooking. 5. No, the kids can't stand doing homework. 6. Yes, Jack loves going to the movies. 7. Yes, Marta likes the opera, but she prefers the theater. 8. Yes, I enjoy watching soccer on television, but I prefer playing soccer. 9. No, Paul doesn't like to play chess very much. 10. Yes, Sam loves inviting friends over for dinner.

✎ Drive It Home

Let's practice this, that, these, and those. Make sentences, following the example.

Example: The car is here. It is new.
Answer: **This car is new.**

1. The book is here. It is boring.

_____

2. The food is here. It is very good.

_____

3. The horse is there. It is beautiful.

_____

4. The kids are there. They are playing on the computer.

_____

5. The people are here. They are watching a football game.

_____

6. We are at the party. It is really boring.

_____

7. We are watching a movie. It is exciting.

_____

8. We do not have the bikes now. They are too expensive.

_____

ANSWER KEY:
1. This book is boring. 2. This food is very good. 3. That horse is beautiful. 4. Those kids are playing on the computer. 5. These people are watching a football game. 6. This party is really boring. 7. This movie is exciting. 8. Those bikes are too expensive.

Hello! How Are You?   Big or Small? Short or Tall?   Everyday Life

This Is My Family   Welcome to My Home!

Parting Words

Well done! You just finished your last lesson of *Essential English*. Do you know:

☐ vocabulary for hobbies and interests? (No? Go back to 203.)

☐ how to talk about what you **like** and what you **don't like**? (No? Go back to 204.)

☐ vocabulary for free time activities? (No? Go back to 207.)

☐ how to use demonstratives like **this** and **that**? (No? Go back to 210.)

☐ how to put it all together in a conversation about weekend plans?
(No? Go back to 212.)

Don't forget to practice and reinforce what you've learned by visiting www.livinglanguage.com/languagelab for flashcards, games, and quizzes!

Word Recall

Let's review some of the important vocabulary from Lesson 10. Fill in the blanks with the missing word or words.

A.

1. I enjoy _____ food and inviting my friends over for dinner.

2. Do you prefer _____ books or magazines?

3. I don't like _____ because I don't like horses.

4. We have a new bike, so tomorrow we're going _____.

B.

1. What are two musical instruments from this lesson?

_____

2. What are two things from this lesson that some people enjoy collecting?

_____

3. What do people enjoy doing on water, for example, in the ocean or on a lake?

_____

4. What do people see at a theater?

_____

Hello! How Are You?   Big or Small? Short or Tall?   Everyday Life

This Is My Family   Welcome to My Home!

5. Where do you go to see romantic comedies, action films, or horror films?

_____

6. What kind of games do people enjoy watching on television?

_____

7. If something isn't boring, it's …

_____

8. What are two games that people play on a table?

_____

ANSWER KEY
A. 1. cooking; 2. reading; 3. horseback riding; 4. biking
B. 1. guitar and piano; 2. stamps and coins; 3. boating; 4. a play; 5. to the movies; 6. football, basketball, baseball, soccer, etc.; 7. exciting; 8. chess, cards

Quiz 2

Let's see how you've done with a short quiz on what you learned in Lessons 6-10. After you've answered all of the questions, score your quiz and see how you did. If you find that you need to go back and review, please do so before continuing on to the review dialogues at the end of this course.

Let's get started!

A. Where do you buy ... ?

1. books, magazine, coffee   a. at an electronics store
2. computers, televisions, stereos b. at a bakery
3. beef and pork   c. at a hardware store
4. bread and cake   d. at a convenience store
5. hammers and paint   e. at a butcher shop

B. Fill in the blanks with some or any.

1. We don't have _____ books in French.

2. I feel like drinking _____ tea.

3. Are there _____ good movies playing this weekend?

4. There aren't _____ nice pants in this store.

5. Please put _____ spinach on my plate.

C. Now fill in with **much** or **many**.

1. How _____ children do you have?

2. I like horseback riding very _____.

3. There aren't _____ good stores at the mall.

4. I don't want too _____ sugar in my coffee.

5. You shouldn't drink so _____ cups of coffee.

D. Give the negative and question forms of the following.

1. They're watching a football game.

   _____

2. Doctors work many hours at the hospital.

   _____

3. He gets to work by bus.

   _____

4. Her assistant eats lunch at twelve thirty.

   _____

5. They feel like cooking tonight.

   _____

E. Choose the right verb form.

1. I (**work/am working**) every weekday.

2. They (**have/are having**) a meeting right now.

3. We (**go/are going**) to the theater tomorrow night.

4. Bob (**speaks/is speaking**) four languages.

5. Architects (**design/are designing**) buildings.

ANSWER KEY

A. 1. d; 2. a; 3. e; 4. b; 5. c

B. 1. any; 2. some; 3. any; 4. any; 5. some

C. 1. many; 2. much; 3. many; 4. much; 5. many

D. 1. They aren't watching a football game. Are they watching a football game? 2. Doctors don't work many hours at the hospital. Do doctors work many hours at the hospital? 3. He doesn't get to work by bus. Does he get to work by bus? 4. Her assistant doesn't eat lunch at twelve thirty. Does her assistant eat lunch at twelve thirty? 5. They don't feel like cooking tonight. Do they feel like cooking tonight?

E. 1. work; 2. are having; 3. are going; 4. speaks; 5. design

How Did You Do?

Give yourself a point for every correct answer, then use the following key to determine whether or not you're ready to move on:

0-10 points: It's probably best to go back and study the lessons again to make sure you understood everything completely. Take your time; it's not a race! Make sure you spend time reviewing the vocabulary and reading through each Grammar Builder section carefully.

11-18 points: If the questions you missed were in section A, you may want to review the vocabulary from previous lessons again; if you missed answers mostly in sections B, C, D, or E, check the Grammar Builder sections to make sure you have your grammar basics down.

19-25 points: You're doing a great job! You're ready to move on to the Review Dialogues!

[   ] **points**

Hello! How Are You? Big or Small? Short or Tall? Everyday Life

This Is My Family Welcome to My Home!

Review Dialogues
Welcome!

Here's your chance to practice all the vocabulary and grammar you've learned in ten lessons of *Living Language Essential English* with these five everyday dialogues. After each dialogue, there are questions to check your understanding. To practice your pronunciation, don't forget to listen to the audio.

There will be words and phrases in these dialogues that you don't know. This is because these are more like "real" English conversations. As usual, use your dictionary to look up words or phrases that you do not know.

🔊 Dialogue 1
▶ 1A Listen (CD 3, Track 21) 1B Listen and Repeat (CD 3, Track 22)

Sarah sits next to Diego on the first day of class. Before class begins, they introduce themselves and talk about their roommates and families.

Sarah:	Hi, I'm Sarah. What's your name?
Diego:	Oh hey. I'm Diego. Nice to meet you. Are you a freshman?
Sarah:	Yes, I am.
Diego:	Me too.
Sarah:	Where are you from?
Diego:	I'm from Puebla, Mexico.
Sarah:	Oh, so you speak Spanish. I speak a little Spanish. I'm from Frankfurt, Germany. Do you speak German?
Diego:	No, I only speak Spanish, English, and a little French. Do you live on campus?

Sarah:	Yes, I live in a dorm room with two roommates, Yuko and Laura. Yuko is from Japan. I don't speak any Japanese, but she speaks English very well. Laura is from New York. Her English is pretty good!
	[laughs]
Diego:	I guess so! Is your dorm room big?
Sarah:	No, it's quite small. And yours?
Diego:	I live in a house with my family. I have two brothers, David and Javier, and one sister, Anna. My brothers are 17 and 19, and my sister is 23. My parents are Luisa and Rogelio. My father is a professor and my mother is an engineer. Is your family big?
Sarah:	Well, not really. I don't have any brothers and sisters, but I have lots of cousins. My father has four brothers and they all live near us.
Diego:	So you live with just your parents?
Sarah:	No, I live with my grandmother and grandfather. My grandmother is 85 years old and my grandfather is 90! My grandmother is from France, so she also speaks French.
Diego:	Oh, here comes the professor.
Sarah:	Let's talk more after class, okay? How about we go to the cafe near the dormitory?
Diego:	Sure!

✎ Dialogue 1 Practice

Now let's check your understanding of the dialogue and review what you learned in Lessons 1-10 of *Essential English*.

Hello! How Are You?   Big or Small? Short or Tall?   Everyday Life

This Is My Family   Welcome to My Home!

A. Give the name of the family member that best completes the sentence.

1. Your uncle's children are your _____.

2. Your mother's mother is your _____.

3. Your mother's father is your _____.

4. Your uncle's wife is your _____.

5. Your father's brother is your _____.

B. For each person listed below, write the country they're from and their nationality. Write two complete sentences. So for example:

(Diego) **Diego is from Mexico. He is Mexican.**

1. Sarah

_____

2. Yuko

_____

3. Laura

_____

4. Sarah's grandmother

_____

C. Answer the questions with the correct person from the dialogue.

1. Who is 23? _____

2. Who speaks Japanese? _____

3. Who is an engineer? _____

4. Who is 90? _____

5. Who has four brothers? _____

ANSWER KEY
A. 1. **cousins**; 2. **grandmother**; 3. **grandfather**; 4. **aunt**; 5. **uncle**
B. 1. **Sarah is from Germany. She is German.** 2. **Yuko is from Japan. She is Japanese.** 3. **Laura is from America. She is American.** 4. **Sarah's grandmother is from France. She is French.**
C. 1. **Diego's sister/Anna**; 2. **Yuko**; 3. **Diego's mother**; 4. **Sarah's grandfather**; 5. **Sarah's father**

𝄞 Dialogue 2
▶ 2A Listen (CD 3, Track 23) 2B Listen and Repeat (CD 3, Track 24)

Listen as Christina describes her parents' home to her friend Bill.

Bill:	**Christina, do you live with your parents?**
Christina:	**Yes, I do. Our house is far from the city center, but it's big and comfortable.**
Bill:	**How many bedrooms are there?**
Christina:	**There are three bedrooms, a living room, a dining room, and a kitchen. In the study, there are lots of books and a computer. I study in there because it is quiet. The kitchen is not big, but it's new. There is a stove, a refrigerator, and a long table.**
Bill:	**Where is your bedroom?**
Christina:	**It's between my parents' bedroom and the study. In my bedroom, there is a bed, a dresser, a bookshelf, and a desk. There are two windows, so it's very sunny.**
Bill:	**Is there a bathroom next to your room?**
Christina:	**No, but there is a bathroom next to my sister's room. There's a shower and a bathtub. The living room is under my parents' bedroom. There's a couch and a television. My dog sleeps on the couch.**
Bill:	**Oh, you have a dog? Do you have a yard?**

Hello! How Are You?   Big or Small? Short or Tall?   Everyday Life

This Is My Family   Welcome to My Home!

Christina:	Yes. The yard is not big, but our dog is small, so it's okay.
Bill:	Do you have a picture of your family?
Christina:	Yes, here. These are my parents and this is my sister.
Bill:	Wow, she really looks like you. But she has long hair and yours is short. Is she a student?
Christina:	No, she works for a company in New York City now. Her name is Ashley. She lives in an apartment there, but she comes home to my parents' house often.
Bill:	That's nice. Okay, I have class now. See you tomorrow!

✎ Dialogue 2 Practice

A. Write the opposite of the adjective used in the dialogue.

1. near _____

2. long _____

3. loud _____

4. old _____

B. Write a yes/no question for each sentence. For example:

The house is far.
Is the house far?

1. The kitchen is sunny.

_____

2. The house has three bedrooms.

_____

3. Christina has a dog.

   _____

4. The dog is small.

   _____

5. Ashley and Christina are sisters.

   _____

C. Match the object with its location.

1. stove	a. bedroom
2. shower	b. living room
3. dresser	c. kitchen
4. computer	d. study
5. couch	e. bathroom

ANSWER KEY

A. 1. far; 2. short; 3. quiet; 4. new

B. 1. Is the kitchen sunny? 2. Does the house have three bedrooms? 3. Does Christina have a dog? 4. Is the dog small? 5. Are Ashley and Christina sisters?

C. 1. c; 2. e; 3. a; 4. d 5. b

ᴄᴄ Dialogue 3

▶ 3A Listen (CD 3, Track 25) 3B Listen and Repeat (CD 3, Track 26)

Sam is visiting his friend Jenny for a few days. Listen as they talk about her routine and her town.

Jenny:	So, Sam, what do you want to do today? I don't have to go to work, so I can hang out all day.
Sam:	Oh, great! Well, what do you usually do on weekends?

Hello! How Are You?   Big or Small? Short or Tall?   Everyday Life

This Is My Family   Welcome to My Home!

Jenny:	Hmm. Well, I get up late, usually around 10 a.m. Then, I shower and get dressed and go to the bakery on the corner.
Sam:	What do you get at the bakery?
Jenny:	I get coffee and a pastry. Sometimes two. They're delicious!
Sam:	And then what do you do?
Jenny:	Well, on Saturday, there is a farmer's market at Hillside Park.
Sam:	Oh, where is that? Is it far?
Jenny:	No, it's not far. It's just a couple of miles away.
Sam:	How do you get there?
Jenny:	I usually go by bus. The market is open until 3 p.m., but people buy all of the best produce by noon.
Sam:	Oh, I see. And then? What do you do next?
Jenny:	After I buy my groceries, I go home and put them away. By then, I'm hungry again! So, I make lunch. Then, I go to the gym with my friend, Emily. She lives across the street. We talk while we exercise. Do you exercise?
Sam:	I do sometimes. But when I'm on vacation, I don't exercise. It's a rule!
Jenny:	I like that rule. Hey, I think there is a good movie showing right now. Do you want to see a movie?
Sam:	Sure. When does it start?
Jenny:	Hm, let's see. There are two showings: at half past one or two forty-five.
Sam:	One thirty sounds good. But first, I want to try those pastries. Are you hungry?
Jenny:	You know me! I'm always hungry!

✎ Dialogue 3 Practice

A. Answer the questions about the dialogue above. Write a full sentence! For example:

What does Jenny eat for breakfast?
She eats pastries.

1. When does Jenny get up on her day off?

   _____

2. Where does Jenny buy coffee?

   _____

3. How does Jenny go to the farmers' market?

   _____

4. Who goes to the gym with Jenny?

   _____

B. Match the numbers for time with the English for time.

1. 10:15	a. **half past eight**
2. 8:30	b. **twelve fifteen**
3. 2:45	c. **noon**
4. 12:15	d. **quarter past ten**
5. 12:00	e. **two forty-five**

ANSWER KEY

A. 1. **She gets up around 10:00 a.m.** 2. **She buys coffee at the bakery.** 3. **Jenny goes to the farmers' market by bus.** 4. **Jenny goes to the gym with her friend, Emily.**

B. 1. d; 2. a; 3. e; 4. b; 5. c

Hello! How Are You?   Big or Small? Short or Tall?   Everyday Life

This Is My Family   Welcome to My Home!

ᴬ Dialogue 4

▶ 4A Listen (CD 3, Track 27) 4B Listen and Repeat (CD 3, Track 28)

Katie needs a dress for a wedding. She goes with her boyfriend, Mark, to a department store in the mall. Mark hates shopping.

Mark: We're going to the department store? Do I have to come? Can I wait in the bookstore for you?

Katie: No, you must come with me. I need your help! Besides, you are going to this wedding, too. You should buy a new jacket. Your old jacket is too small.

Mark: Who is getting married, again? I forget.

Katie: My cousin! She's a doctor, remember? She works at St. Francis Hospital.

Mark: Oh, now I remember. Oh good. I can ask her about my foot problem.

Katie: No, you can't! She is getting married. She doesn't need to talk about your feet that day! Now, which one is prettier, the blue dress or the silver dress?

Mark: How much do they cost?

Katie: The blue dress is cheaper, but the silver dress is nicer. Don't you think?

Mark: I like the blue one.

Katie: Hm. Well, I think the silver one is better. I want to try it on. While I'm trying on the dress, you should look at the jackets. There are lots of different colors and styles.

Mark: I want the most comfortable jacket. And I don't want to spend too much money.

Katie: You can find a jacket like that, I'm sure. And then, we have to buy some shoes and stockings. And a gift!

Mark: Hey, wait. Are you paying for this? I only have a little money.

Katie:	It's fine. I'm paying for it. Now, go to the men's department and choose a jacket. The jacket should be warmer than your old jacket. It's winter. Oh and a belt! Then, we can meet at the cash register.
Mark:	All right. Since you are paying for it, I guess I can't complain.
Katie:	Exactly. Now, go!

✎ Dialogue 4 Practice

A. Write the word from the dialogue in the blank.

1. The blue dress is cheaper but the silver dress is _____.

2. No, you _____ come with me.

3. While I am trying on the dress, you _____ look at the jackets.

4. Now, go to the _____ and choose a jacket.

5. Since you are _____ for it, I guess I can't complain.

B. Write the comparative and superlative form of the adjective.

1. big _____

2. warm _____

3. comfortable _____

4. cheap _____

5. pretty _____

ANSWER KEY
A. 1. nicer; 2. must; 3. should; 4. men's department; 5. paying
B. 1. bigger, biggest; 2. warmer, warmest; 3. more comfortable, most comfortable; 4. cheaper, cheapest; 5. prettier, prettiest

Hello! How Are You?   Big or Small? Short or Tall?   Everyday Life

                   This Is My Family   Welcome to My Home!

◉ Dialogue 5

▶ 5A Listen (CD 3, Track 29) 5B Listen and Repeat (CD 3, Track 30)

Sean and Kara are on a blind date (they are meeting on a date for the first time). They talk about their jobs and hobbies.

Sean:	Is this table okay?
Kara:	Hm, how about that table? It's quieter over there.
Sean:	Sure! So, tell me about yourself. What do you do?
Kara:	Well, I'm an office manager. So, you know, I organize the office: schedule meetings, buy supplies, and direct phone calls and emails. I work from nine to five on weekdays. I like my job a lot. My boss is really nice. She's an architect. What about you? What do you do?
Sean:	I'm a cook at a restaurant. I love making new dishes, so it's very exciting. But I don't like the schedule. I work from four o'clock until midnight. And I have to work on weekends.
Kara:	Oh, that's too bad. But shouldn't you be at work right now? It's seven o'clock.
Sean:	No, I don't work on Mondays. It's my night off. And here I am, in a restaurant!
Kara:	Yeah, I guess you can't escape it! Well, tonight you don't have to cook at least.
Sean:	That's true. What do you usually do on weekends? Do you have any hobbies?
Kara:	I love to play soccer, so I often go to the park and play a game with my friends. Do you play soccer?
Sean:	No, but I love watching it. Do you have any other hobbies?
Kara:	I like going to the movies a lot.
Sean:	Me too! Do you feel like seeing a movie this weekend? I finish work early, around six o'clock.
Kara:	That sounds great! What do you prefer: horror movies, romantic comedies, science fiction … ?

Let's Eat! | At Work | **Review Dialogues**

Around Town | Let's Go Shopping | What Do You Feel Like Doing?

Sean: I don't like romantic comedies or science fiction, but I love watching horror movies.

Kara: Me too! Perfect. The Claw is playing this weekend, I think. Do you want to see that?

Sean: Yeah! Oh, here comes the waiter. We should look at the menu. Do you know what you want?

Kara: I want a cheeseburger, with French fries.

Sean: Me too! What a coincidence. I feel like we have a lot in common. Don't you?

Kara: Yes, I do, too.

✎ Dialogue 5 Practice

A. Write a sentence using present progressive tense to describe what Sean and Kara are doing.

Example: It's Sunday afternoon. Sean (to watch a soccer game)
Answer: Sean is watching a soccer game.

1. It's 7:30 p.m. Sean (to work)

   _____

2. It's 5 p.m. on Monday. Kara (to leave her office)

   _____

3. It's Monday night. Sean and Kara (to have dinner)

   _____

4. It's Saturday night. Sean and Kara (to watch a horror movie)

   _____

Hello! How Are You? Big or Small? Short or Tall? Everyday Life

This Is My Family Welcome to My Home!

5. It's Sunday afternoon. Kara and her friends (to play soccer)

_____

B. Choose the best ending to the sentence.

1. Kara is ...

   a. a teacher.

   b. an engineer.

   c. an architect.

   d. an office manager.

2. Sean doesn't like ...

   a. to watch soccer.

   b. to watch horror movies.

   c. his schedule.

   d. cheeseburgers.

3. Sean ...

   a. works on Mondays.

   b. hates his job.

   c. loves science fiction.

   d. likes making new dishes.

ANSWER KEY
A. 1. Sean is working. 2. Kara is leaving her office. 3. Sean and Kara are having dinner. 4. Sean and Kara are watching a horror movie. 5. Kara and her friends are playing soccer.
B. 1. d; 2. c; 3. d

Grammar Summary

1. ARTICLES

	SINGULAR	PLURAL
definite	the boy	the boys
indefinite (starts with vowel sound)	an hour*	--
indefinite (starts with consonant sound)	a girl	--

*Notice that we say an hour but a house. Listen to the first sound; do not rely only on spelling. The h is silent in hour.

2. PLURAL NOUNS

a. Most nouns add –s in the plural.

one boy	two boys
one girl	two girls

b. If a word ends in a consonant + –y, change –y to –ie and add –s.

one university	two universities

c. Some plurals are irregular:

one man	two men
one woman	three women
one child	four children
one person	ten people

3. THE VERB TO BE

a. Here are the forms of to be in present tense in full and then contracted forms.

	SINGULAR	PLURAL
1st person	I am (I'm)	we are (we're)
2nd person	you are (you're)	you are (you're)

	SINGULAR	PLURAL
3rd person	he is, she is, it is (he's, she's, it's)	they are (they're)

b. Here are the contracted forms of **to be** + **not**.

	SINGULAR	PLURAL
1st person	I am not = I'm not	we are not = we're not or we aren't
2nd person	you are not = you're not or you aren't	you are not = you're not or you aren't
3rd person	he/she/it is not = he isn't, she isn't, it isn't or he's not, she's not, it's not	they are not = they're not or they aren't

4. THE VERB TO HAVE

	SINGULAR	PLURAL
1st person	I have	we have
2nd person	you have	you have
3rd person	he has, she has, it has	they have

5. NEGATION WITH TO HAVE AND OTHER VERBS:

a. With **have** + **not**, use **do/does** + **not have**. Here are the full and contracted forms:

	SINGULAR	PLURAL
1st person	I do not have = I don't have	we do not have = we don't have
2nd person	you do not have = you don't have	you do not have = you don't have
3rd person	he/she/it does not have = he/she/it doesn't have	they do not have = they don't have

b. The pattern is the same for other verbs (except to be):

The boys don't eat ...
The boy doesn't like ...

6. POSSESSION

a. Possessive pronouns

	SINGULAR	PLURAL
1st person	my	our
2nd person	your	your
3rd person	his, her, its	their

b. You can also express possession with 's, as in Laura's brother, and Billy and Jenny's cousin

7. YES/NO QUESTIONS

a. To ask a yes/no question with am, is, or are, move the verb to the front.

He is Chinese.	Is he Chinese?

b. To answer a yes/no question with am, is, or are, use yes, or no + not.

Is he Chinese?	Yes, he is. or No, he isn't./No, he's not.

c. To ask a question with have or has, use do/does ... have?

They have a dog.	Do they have a dog?
She has a dog.	Does she have a dog?
They work at the school.	Do they work at the school?
She works at the bank.	Does she work at the bank?

d. To answer a question with **have** or **has** or another verb like **work**, use **yes** or **no** + **do not have**.

Do they have children?	–Yes, they <u>have</u> children. –No, they <u>do not have</u> children.
Does Bob have a wife?	–Yes, he <u>has</u> a wife. –No, he <u>does not have</u> a wife.
Do they work at the school?	–No, they <u>don't work</u> at the school. –Yes, they <u>work</u> at the school.
Does she work at the bank?	–No, she <u>doesn't work</u> at the bank. –Yes, she <u>works</u> at the bank.

8. QUESTION WORDS

what?	<u>What</u> does John do in the morning? He <u>eats breakfast</u> in the morning.
who?	<u>Who</u> do the students see in class? They see <u>their professor</u> in class.
when?	<u>When</u> does the train leave? The train leaves <u>at 9:05 in the morning</u>.
where?	<u>Where</u> do Bill and Cynthia live? They live <u>in Chicago</u>.
how?	<u>How</u> do you get to work? I get to work <u>by bus</u>.
why?	<u>Why</u> do you buy bread at the bakery? I buy bread at the bakery <u>because it is good</u>.

9. CARDINAL NUMBERS

one, two, three	1, 2, 3

four, five, six	4, 5, 6
seven, eight	7, 8
nine, ten	9, 10
eleven, twelve, thirteen	11, 12, 13
fourteen, fifteen, sixteen	14, 15, 16
seventeen, eighteen, nineteen	17, 18, 19
twenty, thirty, forty	20, 30, 40
fifty, sixty, seventy	50, 60, 70
eighty, ninety, one hundred	80, 90, 100
twenty–one, twenty–two, twenty–three	21, 22, 23
thirty–four, thirty–five, thirty–six	34, 35, 36
forty–seven, fifty–eight, ninety–nine	47, 58, 99

10. ORDINAL NUMBERS

first, second, third, fourth	1st, 2nd, 3rd, 4th
fifth, sixth, seventh, eighth	5th, 6th, 7th, 8th
ninth, tenth, eleventh, twelfth	9th, 10th, 11th, 12th

11. THERE IS/THERE ARE

| There is + singular noun | There are + plural noun |
| There is a desk in the room. | There are desks in the room. |

12. COMMON PREPOSITIONS

in	We live in a house.
on	The books are on the bookshelf.
from	Ram is from India.

next to	The chair is <u>next to</u> the table.
near	New York is <u>near</u> Philadelphia.
far from	Los Angeles is <u>far from</u> New York.
under	The cat is <u>under</u> the couch.
between	The bathroom is <u>between</u> the bedroom and the kitchen.

13. VERBS IN PRESENT TENSE

a. Most verbs add –s to he, she, and it forms.

I work	we work
you work	you work
He works, she works, it works	they work

b. Verbs that end in –ch, –sh, –x, –z, –s and –o, add –es in the he, she, and it forms. Verbs that end in –y take –ies in the he, she, and it form.

watch/watches	He watches TV at night.
do/does	The student does her homework.
study/studies	John studies English literature at the university.

14. VERBS IN PRESENT PROGRESSIVE

a. Use am, is, or are + verb +–ing.

I am working	we are working
you are working	you are working
he/she/it is working	they are working

b. In the negative, put not before the verb.

I am not eating	we are not eating
you are not eating	you are not eating

Essential English

he/she/it is not eating	they are not eating

15. POLITE REQUESTS

please + verb (no ending)	Please bring me the menu.
could you + verb (no ending)?	Could you bring me the menu?
subject + would like	I would like a menu.

16. DEMONSTRATIVES

	SINGULAR	PLURAL
near to speaker	This is my bicycle. I like this bicycle. I like this one.	These are my bicycles. I like these bicycles. I like these ones.
far from speaker	That is my bicycle. I like that bicycle. I like that one.	Those are my bicycles. I like those bicycles. I like those ones.

17. SOME AND ANY

amounts that aren't specific or exact	some water, some time
things that you can count (in plural)	some people, some tables
in questions in which the subject is indefinite	Would you like some vegetables?
in negative (not) sentences	I don't have any bread.
in questions	Would you like any vegetables?

18. QUANTITY EXPRESSIONS

ask about things you count	how many people?
ask about things you don't count	how much money?

negative	There are no people at the store.
	There aren't any people at the store.
a small amount of things you count	I have a few books.
a small amount of things you do not count	I only spend a little money on food.
a big amount	I have a lot of books
	I have lots of books.
	I have many books.
more than enough	You spend too much time shopping!
	You have too many cats!

19. THE COMPARATIVE AND SUPERLATIVE

a. To make a comparative add –er to short adjectives. To make a superlative add –est.

old	Older
	I am older than you, but he is older than me.
	He is the oldest.

b. Spelling changes and irregulars

big	bigger/biggest
happy	happier/happiest
good	better/best
bad	worse/worst

c. Long adjectives use **more** instead of –er for the comparative and **most** instead of –est for the superlative.

difficult	**more/most difficult**
	Algebra is more difficult than geometry; calculus is more difficult than algebra.
	Calculus is the most difficult.

d. The opposite of more is less, and the opposite of the most is the least.

difficult	**less/least difficult**
	Algebra is less difficult than calculus, but geometry is less difficult than algebra.
	Geometry is the least difficult.

20. THE VERBS WANT TO, HAVE TO, CAN, MUST, SHOULD, AND NEED TO

to express desire	**want/wants + to + verb**
	do/does + not (don't/doesn't) + want + to
to express ability	**can + verb**
	cannot/can't + verb
to express obligation	**have + to + verb**
	do/does + not + (don't/doesn't) + have + to + verb (Careful! This expresses choice not obligation in negative.)
	must + verb
	must + not (mustn't) + verb

to express a suggestion	should + verb
	should + not (shouldn't) + verb
to express necessity or obligation	need + to + verb
	do/does + not (don't/doesn't) + need + to + verb